The Class Matrix

The Class Matrix

Social Theory after the Cultural Turn

Vivek Chibber

HARVARD UNIVERSITY PRESS

Cambridge, Massachusetts & London, England

2022

Second printing

Library of Congress Cataloging-in-Publication Data

Names: Chibber, Vivek, 1965– author.
Title: The class matrix : social theory after the cultural turn / Vivek
Chibber.
Description: Cambridge, Massachusetts : Harvard University Press, 2022. |
Includes bibliographical references and index.
Identifiers: LCCN 2021016804 | ISBN 9780674245136 (cloth)
Subjects: LCSH: Social classes. | Class consciousness. | Wealth—Social
aspects. | Materialism—Social aspects. | Equality.
Classification: LCC HT609 .C49 2022 | DDC 305.5—dc23
LC record available at https://lccn.loc.gov/2021016804

For Erik Olin Wright

In Memorium

Contents

A Note on Terminology

One of the most frequently used concepts in this book is "culture." Among contemporary theorists, the concept is understood in two distinct ways. One tradition, associated perhaps most famously with Raymond Williams, takes it to mean an entire "way of life"—the gamut of social practices that distinguish one social formation or one epoch from another. This includes not only religion, ideology, the arts, and literature but also political and economic institutions. Another, more narrow use of the term uses it to denote ideology, discourse, normative codes, and so on—together comprising the interpretive dimension of social practices. In this book, unless otherwise noted, I will always use "culture" and its cognates in the *latter* sense. There is a reason for this. One of the primary goals of the book is to respond to the challenges to structural class theory issued by proponents of the "cultural turn." That challenge only makes sense if "culture" is understood in this particular way—as will be clear in the course of the book. It is a practical decision, not an epistemological stance. Readers who feel strongly that the concept should not be used in this fashion can feel free to substitute "ideology" or "discourse" whenever they see "culture." I usually use them interchangeably.

The Class Matrix

Introduction

One of the enduring problems in social theory is to explain the sources of stability and conflict in modern society. For most of the twentieth century, perhaps the most influential approach to this issue originated in the work of Karl Marx. Marx's arguments directly or indirectly shaped much of the debate on modern political dynamics. Marx's direct influence came through his empirical arguments, the most important of which was that stability and conflict don't just coexist but are coextensive. It isn't just that modern society has both elements within it but that they are produced together. This is because the same mechanism that brings people into stable patterns of interaction also locks them into conflict with one another. Marx often described this situation through the concept of "contradiction" and its cognates—not in the sense of a logical impossibility but of an irreconcilable tension.

For Marx, the mechanism that simultaneously produces stability and conflict is the class structure. On one side, a society's class relations create the foundation for its reproduction over time. This is because, by definition, these are the social relations that govern the production of goods and services. Whatever else people might do, they have to participate in the forms of interaction called for by the class structure just to maintain body and soul. A society's class structure is therefore a source of social stability because the social agents are inclined to reproduce it as the precondition for their own well-being. On the other side, though, it is also the primary source of social tension. This is because class is intrinsically exploitative—dominant classes obtain their income by coercing labor out of subordinate groups. Marx refers to this labor extraction as exploitation, and exploitation is built into the process of class reproduction. So even while the class structure brings social agents together around their material needs, it also locks them into conflict because exploitation tends to generate resistance. In his most famous articulation of this argument, Marx predicted that the political instability built into capitalism would eventuate in its overthrow by the working class.

It was no small matter that in the decades following Marx's demise, most of Europe was rocked by working-class rebellions, and there seemed a very real possibility that his prediction of capitalism's demise would come true. Socialist parties turned to Marxism as their guide to action, and as tens of millions flocked to these organizations, they imbibed the basics of the theory. By mid-century, Marxism in some form was undoubtedly the most widely held social theory among progressive intellectuals and exercised great influence beyond. In the colonial world, a similar process took root wherein nationalist movements took inspiration from Marx's anticolonialism and the strong anti-imperialist stance taken by the Bolsheviks. Generations of anticolonial intellectuals found Marxism to provide a natural framework, not just for their moral commitments but also for their political analysis. Hence, for the global Left, the theory's basic elements had become a kind of common sense by the 1960s. And the explosion of the New Left at the decade's end only breathed new life into it, extending its reach far into the academy for the first time.

This is all very well known. It is also widely recognized that as the Left began to weaken and then retreat in the 1970s, it triggered an intellectual crisis. Whereas Marx's theory seemed to be in line with the growth of class movements and the threats posed to capitalist rule, the system's stabilization in the latter part of the century, the onset of neoliberal hegemony, the domestication of the organized Left, and the disintegration of the Soviet Bloc all pushed in the opposite direction. All these developments seemed not only to run against the theory's predictions, but, more importantly, it appeared to be ill-equipped to explain them. The anomalies were hard to miss—if the working class was to be capitalism's gravedigger, then how was its ascent, which seemed ineluctable in the century's early decades, halted by mid-century? And on its heels, how and why did so many workers acquiesce to Reagan and Thatcher, who were so obviously committed to elite interests? Why were workers so attracted to racist and xenophobic ideologies when they were supposed to unite around their common interests?

The Left's traditional understanding of class increasingly came into doubt, and the doubts reached ever deeper into the theory's core. They began with Marx's expectations regarding class formation— that is, the process by which actors engage in collective action around their economic interests. Marx famously described the two moments as going from a "class in itself" to a "class for itself." His theory implied a smooth, even inevitable process by which people in the same structural location would come together and fight for their common interests. This apparent determinism about the class structure now came to be seen as the theory's weak point. Classes might be easy to define and even locate as economic actors structurally—as "classes on paper," in Pierre Bourdieu's terminology.[1] But there was no reason to think they would necessarily congeal as political entities. Marx vastly underestimated the contingency of this process, and because of that, he never adequately theorized the mechanisms that actually govern the transformation of class interests into class struggle.

And what were the mechanisms he left out? The one that very quickly rose to the top was *culture*. Marx's theory rested on two propositions: first, that actors' class location generated a set of material interests, and second, that these interests would motivate those actors' political strategy. But even if the first claim were true, the second raised a host of problems. Chief among these was that, in order to serve as a motive for action, interests had to be perceived in the appropriate way by the actors. But this process—of perceiving and understanding their material interests—was necessarily mediated by the symbolic universe the actors inhabited. Class interests would only become politically operative if they were translated into the appropriate cultural codes.

This argument was the first step in what has come to be known as "the cultural turn." It initiated a tectonic shift in social analysis toward the important role of ideas and meaning in class formation and later in social relations more generally. And the payoff in its early years was very exciting. The empirical challenge was to trace the myriad pathways by which the raw economic facts of exploitation and domination were perceived by workers phenomenologically. No work of historical scholarship exemplified this agenda more clearly, and more brilliantly, than Edward Thompson's *The Making of the English Working Class*.[2] Thompson's book was in some part a work of excavation—as he explained, a project to recover ordinary workers "from the enormous condescension of posterity."[3] But more importantly, it also held the promise of solving an analytical dilemma—of explicating the mechanisms that comprised the link between economic interests and social action. For the emerging New Left in the 1960s and 1970s, the investigation of popular culture—of the formation of class consciousness—was exciting because it would unlock the secret to class formation.

This version of the cultural turn was, in many respects, an innovation *within* traditional Marxism. It took culture as the mechanism that helped explain the vicissitudes of class formation. But it did not question the basic integrity of the class structure in the economy, and it did not doubt that the structure really generated class interests. What culture did was enable, or in other cases block, the translation of those economic interests in a way that resonated with the actors' emotional universe. When the role was positive, it created an awareness of one's location in the class structure and the interests that derived from it. When it was negative, it blocked the formation of this consciousness and instead facilitated the integration of the working class into the economic system. Indeed, the early works coming from the Marxist camp, which later were enshrined as the progenitors of the cultural turn, never doubted the reality of class structure or the interests it generated.

But the implications soon spilled over into the theorization of class structure itself. Once it was admitted that culture mediated the impact of interests on politics, the question naturally arose, why just politics? If their ideology, religion, or language mediates the sorts of political choices actors make, why won't it also filter how they understand their economic choices? People don't split their time between engaging in economy for part of the day, where culture is banned, and in political activities during the rest of it, where culture is allowed to roam free. But, of course, this is exactly what the classical Marxist metaphor of the base and superstructure seemed to suggest. The base referred to the economic foundation of society—its class structure—and the superstructure was the domain of politics, culture, law, and such. The model seemed to divide society into two parts, and the part where the class structure was located was declared a culture-free zone.

Class theory had to recognize that constellations of meaning—how actors subjectively interpreted their situation—were involved in every kind of social action and, therefore, in every social structure, including class. And once it was imported into the consideration of class structure, the implications of the cultural turn were profound. In its earlier phase, scholars had assumed that Marx's arguments regarding the economic structure were basically sound; the problem resided in his putative determinism about how the structure related to political agency. Now the destabilizing effect of culture was extended to the class structure itself. Three shifts in the theorization of structure were especially significant.

The first change was in the proposed relation between class structure and interests. The classical theory had assumed a stable relationship between class as a structure and the material interests generated by it. The entire premise of class analysis was that it was possible to predict actors' economic strategies on the basis of their location in the structure. But the introduction of culture now undermined the notion that structures could be identified with a stable set of interests. As Patrick Joyce, a leading theorist of the cultural turn, argued, "interests are not somehow given in the economic condition of workers but are *constructed through the agency* of *social identities*."[4] When classical Marxists suggested that workers' economic condition would impel them into revolutionary activity, they supposed that workers' identity is an effect of their class position. Joyce expresses the widely

held sentiment that the causal chain runs in the opposite direction—
it is through the prism of their pregiven identities that actors come
to understand their location in the structure. Furthermore, culture
generates an irreducible *contingency* to how structures generate action.
Again from Joyce, "economic relationships, however exploitative, . . .
present themselves to people in *countless ways*, conditioned by culture
and circumstance." The same structural location can therefore motivate very different forms of social action, depending on how local
constellations of meaning shape their perception of the action. This
being the case, there is no straight line leading from one to the other.
Joyce concludes that once the centrality of meaning is recognized,
"the [very] language of interests breaks down."[5]

But if interests generated by class structure are so powerfully
shaped by culture, then why not the structure itself? This was the
second significant shift. Once it was suggested that culture shaped
how actors perceived their location in the structure, it was a small
step to conclude that the structure itself was the *product* of culture.
Clifford Geertz offered a heuristic that articulated many theorists'
intuitions on the matter. In his celebrated essay "Notes on a Javanese
Cockfight," Geertz suggested that the interplay of roles in the popular game was a kind of social structure.[6] Participants related to one
another other in a relational manner, and their pattern of interaction
was governed by a set of rules—much as the relata in a class structure. But in the case of the cockfight, in order for the participants to
properly enact their roles within that structure, they first had to *learn*
what it demanded of them. Their socialization into the appropriate
value orientation was a precondition to the structure being viable at
all. People can't just be placed in each other's proximity and expected
to spontaneously interact as demanded by their roles. They have to
first learn the rules. They have to understand what it means to be a

participant in the game. Meaning construction, therefore, has to be seen as a precondition for people's participation in the structure at all. But if this is so, then once again, culture cannot be viewed as a consequence of structure but as its causal antecedent.

And once culture took its place as the foundation of social structure, it led naturally to a skepticism toward theories claiming universal scope—or "grand narratives," in the preferred jargon of the time. Since cultures are variable across regions, the forms of social practice that they generate will also vary. Actors will be motivated by different values and desires, read their circumstances in highly differentiated ways, and inhabit very diverse social identities. But the variation extends into the various cultures themselves. Whatever their normative socialization happens to be, actors could never blindly follow it in the manner of a script because they cannot. They have to continually imaginatively modify the norms they have been taught as they try to figure out how those norms apply to the specific situation in which they find themselves. Since these innumerable acts of reinterpretation happen locally and will be unpredictable, exactly how a cultural frame will generate social action cannot be taken for granted. It becomes a contingent issue to be discovered through empirical investigation and not prejudged in the manner of Parsonian functionalism. To understand how social context impels action, then, requires that we dispense with universalizing generalizations and attend instead to the specific context—the local site—in which the action is being carried out.

Locality, contingency, and meaning construction—these have been three pillars of the cultural turn. Their elevation has profound implications for social theory. Whereas in the earlier and less ambitious versions of the cultural turn, the challenge was to understand how people located in the same structure could come together as a political force, in the more ambitious version, the question itself appears as confused. It presumes that there is a structure prior to, and independent of, the political and cultural facts of society. But how can there be if structures are themselves linguistically constituted and riven through with contingency and agential autonomy? Indeed, the very idea of an economic *system* seems rather quaint. It requires imputing to social practices a determinacy they simply do not have and, in so doing, suppresses all the contingencies in social reproduction. Thus, politics after the culture turn is unmoored from any underlying economic interests or capacities. It becomes fundamentally open ended—built around identities rather than interests, volition rather than capacities, perception rather than economic facts.

The Global Shift

It is ironic that the embrace of radical contingency, the turn away from economic structure, the skepticism of grand narratives—all this was overtaking social theory precisely at the time when capitalism's remorseless logic was imposing itself around the globe. The cultural turn's denial of independent economic facts is concurrent with what we now call neoliberal globalization. Two components of this neoliberal era have been common across much of the world, both in the North and the South. The first is that the scope of private enterprise has expanded exponentially compared to the first thirty years after World War II. In the aftermath of the war, capitalism expanded its circuits at a steady pace. But it was hampered by several factors. For one thing, much of the Global South was still dominated by peasant production, which presented a natural barrier to the deepening of capitalist social relations. Second, in the advanced industrial world and also in the South, a considerable portion of the economy was dominated by the public sector, hence limiting the economic and political influence of private capital. And third is the obvious fact that around one-third of the world's population lived in centrally planned economies and hence outside scope of capitalist commodity production.

These phenomena acted as powerful barriers to capitalism's grip on global social relations for most of the century. But by the fin de siècle, they had all been considerably weakened. First, the closing decades of the century witnessed a rapid acceleration of the depeasantization underway in the Global South. This was sharpest in Latin America, where the weight of the rural sector in total employment shrank from 50–60 percent of the labor force in 1960 to less than 15 percent on average by 2020.[7] Just as significantly, there was a transformation of the agrarian occupational structure so that the nature of employment shifted away from peasant smallholdings to rural wage labor—marking the absorption of agriculture into capitalist forms. But even outside Latin America, the same process was underway, even if it did not proceed at the same pace.

Within the capitalist world, there was a retreat of the public sector so that lines hitherto closed off to private ownership were now thrown open as part of the global liberalization process. In the Global South, massive state enterprises were auctioned off, or just given away, to private interests; even sectors like power and roads, which at mid-century had been viewed as beyond the capacity of capitalist management, were opened up to capital. In the core capitalist countries, goods and services that had been distributed as citizenship rights were fenced off and turned into commodities. Income supports were weakened or extinguished, and job security rolled back, making most of the population ever more dependent on the labor market for their economic welfare.

And, of course, with the fall of the Soviet Bloc on one side and the marketization of the Chinese economy on the other, close to one-third of humanity was thrown into the vortex of commodity production. Its most immediate and visible effect was a massively deepened dependence on the market in those very parts of the world. Of course, the flip side of this was a correspondingly massive social power for commodity producers—the newly minted capitalists in Eastern Europe and China. Where private property had been extinguished for more than a half century, it not only reemerged but did so in gangster form and at a scale that rivaled the economic power of small nations. But a second, and more portentous, consequence of the collapse of state socialism was the entry of its workers into the capitalist labor market on a scale perhaps hitherto unseen in human history. Within the span of a decade, more than a billion workers joined the global working class and, in so doing, placed immediate downward pressure on wages across the capitalist world.

These trends were essential to the qualitative leap in the scope and weight of private enterprise during the last quarter of the twentieth century. Their cumulative effect was to massively increase the market's power over the lives of billions. And this generated the second great fact about the neoliberal era—a dramatic shift in the political balance between labor and capital, not just in Eastern Europe or the United States but across continents. Even as the capitalist world came out of the decade-long stagnation of the 1970s and early 1980s, the recovery did not witness a rebound in wage growth, as would be expected. In the context of a capitalist class riding high on its recent advances, and a working class absorbing hundreds of millions into its ranks while facing anemic employment growth, unions began a steady retreat over most issues. Starting in the 1980s and even more so in the next decade, organized labor across the world turned increasingly to a defensive strategy, trying merely to hang on to the gains won in previous years rather than pushing for a share of the expanding economic pie.

But the strategy was largely a failure. With labor's organizational strength weakened, a retreat on the distributive front followed soon thereafter. Employment protections shrank both in their scale and, more importantly, in their scope—covering fewer and fewer sections of the labor force. So too with benefits and pension plans. And most pointedly, the share of income going to labor went into decline, presenting the most direct evidence of the shift in political balance. As many studies of income distribution have shown, labor's share of national income has been shrinking across the Organisation for Economic Co-operation and Development (OECD) and many countries in the South for more than two decades.[8] Hence, all across the advanced capitalist world, the neoliberal era witnessed a dramatic shift in the power balance between labor and capital, expressed in a quite diverse mix of empirical measures.

These developments all embodied the same principle—a vast increase in the scope of capital's reach and structural power. They occurred across the world in countries with very distinct cultures, different histories, divergent institutional assemblages, and different forms of government. The subordination to capital was expressed in two distinct but related ways. First was the fact that vast swathes of the working population now had no choice but to conform to its most basic requirements—offering up their labor power to privately owned firms or taking control of these firms and pursuing a profit-maximizing strategy. This was simply a subordination to the impersonal power of the market. The second way it was expressed was in the increased power of the capitalist *class*—both socially and politically. Whereas the first simply announced the universalization of the commodity form as the basic unit of economic activity, the second ensured that all this activity would be carried out to the over-whelming benefit of a tiny section of the population—the owners of wealth and capital.

The Worm Turns

While the structural reach and power of the capitalist market were spreading remorselessly across the globe, the cultural turn continued apace, beating the drum of contingency and agency, as if nothing had happened. It is no surprise that by the early 2000s, there was a growing sense that things had gone too far and that social theory had lost touch with reality. Hence, William Sewell, one of the most influential proponents of the turn to culture in the 1980s, could lament in 2005:

> I have increasingly come to worry that the triumph of cultural his-tory over social history has perhaps been too easy—that . . . impor-tant concepts, especially the fundamental social-historical notion of social structure, have been abandoned almost without argument.

And he noted the irony as well:

> During the very period when historians have gleefully cast aside the notion of structural determination, the shape of our own social world has been fundamentally transformed by changes in the struc-ture of world capitalism.[9]

Sewell's warning was directed at the rarified world of academic production, where there was still very little interest in a recalibration of the theoretical compass. But in the broader culture, things were beginning to change. Even before the publication of his essay, a global mobilization against the inequities of neoliberalism—more massive than anything witnessed in two decades—had broken out. It was ostensibly directed at the Bretton Woods institutions—the International Monetary Fund (IMF) and the World Bank—but its more fundamental target was the very form in which capital was spreading around the world. The movement was derailed by the attacks of 9 / 11 but resurfaced by the end of the decade. And then, in 2011, came the dramatic explosion of the Occupy Wall Street movement, which not only carried forward the attack on inequality but linked the maldistribution of income to the structural logic of capitalism itself. For the first time since the early 1970s, there was a mass social movement aiming its critique at capitalism itself, not just poverty or inequality. This was followed almost immediately by the Arab Spring, which again foregrounded basic economic demands and prominently featured slogans directed at neoliberalism, and then, four years later, the sudden ascension of Bernie Sanders in the United States and Jeremy Corbyn in England, stalwarts of the traditional Left, who gave political expression to the growing movement against the pathologies of this new Gilded Age.

These movements were articulating a growing sensibility that there was something profoundly wrong in the political culture—that the state was captured by the wealthy—and this, in turn, was enabled by the very structure of contemporary capitalism even while social theory was, as Sewell accurately described it, dismissing these connections "more of less out of hand."[10] But the disjuncture between the political environment and the intellectual world could not last forever. Around the same time as the Occupy movement took off, a new wave of scholarship started to make its way into the public, turning the pendulum back to the systemic forces propelling the shift in power and wealth over the past decades.

No doubt the most significant work in this new trend was Thomas Piketty's *Capital in the 21st Century*. It is not often that a 700-page work of dense economic analysis, with a technical apparatus typically confined to specialist journals, captures the popular imagination. With a title that conspicuously harkened back to Marx's great work, Piketty's book sold more than 2.5 million copies within two years of its release. And even though it is quite likely that few of its readers have waded through it cover to cover, they nonetheless fastened onto the basic message the book was intended to convey—that there are enduring structural facts about the capitalist economy and that these facts ensure the flow of income and wealth is preponderantly captured by a narrow economic elite. And with this very simple argument, Piketty revived a message that had once been the staple of critical theory, which seemed now to have little interest in it. But it was not just Piketty. Across the social sciences and humanities, it is common to observe leading scholars announcing the revival of capitalism as an anchor for social analysis.[II] There is a return to the idea that modern society is in some way constrained by the structural properties of capitalism, regardless of culture and across diverse regions.

This Book

A revived concern with the structure of capitalism is to be welcomed, but to return to the status quo ante—to resume a theorization of class structure as if the turn to culture had never happened—would be a mistake. There are many reasons the cultural turn took hold as fiercely as it did, but one of them surely is that its challenges to structural class theory were real. It was, in fact, true that classical Marxism radically undertheorized the sources of stability in capitalism. And this was indeed due, in part, to a determinism in many of its pronouncements regarding class formation. Any viable theory of capitalism will have to remedy these weaknesses. Furthermore, materialists have to provide an answer to the most profound and destabilizing challenge from the cultural turn—if participation in a structure requires the construction of a specific meaning orientation, how can we attribute explanatory primacy to the structure and not to culture? How is materialism even possible if all social action is motivated by meaning and the latter is an effect of culture? To point airily in the direction of global profit shares, declining wage levels, and similar economic patterns is not enough. We need to explain how structural logics are even possible once the ubiquity of culture is admitted. And once we revive a structural theory, what is the place of contingency within it? Culturalists may have overestimated its scope, but surely a revitalized structuralism cannot simply evacuate it. We need to appreciate the limits of structural determination, the point at which outcomes are dictated not by structural facts but by other causal forces.

This book develops a theory of class structure and class formation by way of response to the cultural turn. It is written with the conviction that the road back to materialism goes *through* culture, not around it. For that reason, I engage many of the central objections that cultural theorists have leveled at the materialist tradition. But it is important to note that I only take up these theories where it seems necessary to confront them. This book is not, therefore, a wholesale engagement with theories of culture—it engages them where the explication of my own argument seems to require it. My intention, of course, is to defend the intendent power of economic structures and material interests in key domains. But I try to show that a revitalized structural class theory does not have to ignore the role of meaning and identity. Even more, I affirm culture's centrality in many spheres. So, too, with contingency, agency, and the limits to universalism. In all these instances, my argument is that a robust structural theory of capitalism is useful precisely because it helps us better locate the *place* of culture and contingency in social reproduction. It enables us to understand where culture is decisive and where its force is subordinated to material interests; to see where the force of structural factors ends and, hence, other social forces settle the course of events; and to decipher which properties of capitalism are in fact universalized and which are left to the local and the particular.

The first task is to restore the independent force of economic structure. Here, the challenge from culture is that all structures are subordinate to constellations of meaning. Chapter 1 shows that it is possible to accept the premise that all social relations are *steeped in* culture while rejecting the conclusion that they are therefore causally *subordinate to* it. Indeed, I suggest that in the case of class, we can affirm the very opposite—that the meaning orientation of the actors is causally dependent on their structural location. The peculiarity of class resides in the fact that it is the only social relation that directly governs the material well-being of its participants. Because it has a direct bearing on their welfare, it motivates them to learn and internalize the meanings required to participate in their structural location. Hence, a wage laborer might be new to the idea of having to enter the labor market. But he will quickly appreciate that if he wants to survive, he will have to understand the cultural content of certain practices—finding a job, working for a certain number of hours, developing the skills needed, and so forth. He may not have experience in these practices—they may be phenomenologically alien—but the very fact that his wage is now his lifeline will impel him to acquire cultural competency in them. He is compelled to adjust his meaning orientation to his structural location. The causal arrow thus runs *from* the class structure *to* the meaning orientation of its actors.

Having vindicated the causal priority of class structure over its cultural trappings, I turn in Chapter 2 to the problem of class formation.

In classical Marxism, there was a simple connection between the two—the class structure generates a conflict of interests between capitalists and workers, which motivates workers to create organizations for collective action, with which they eventually overthrow the system. The theory thus seems committed to a very deterministic account of class formation. How is possible to revive the classical theory of the class structure without its obviously false political predictions?

I argue that classical Marxists misunderstood the implications of their own theory. A structural class theory, properly understood, does not predict the inevitability of class formation but rather its uncertainty. The essence of my argument is that capitalism does generate a conflict of interests, as Marx argued. And it also motivates workers to resist their domination, again as Marx suggested. But it makes it more attractive to resist that domination on an *individual* basis, as opposed to a *collective* one. Marx's error was not in assuming the reality of objective interests or predicting resistance. It was in assuming that the *form* of this resistance would most likely be collective.

Once we allow that there is no garden path ensuring that resistance will be collective, as opposed to individual, we can attend to the factors that enable the transition from one to the other. And here, it turns out that culture and subjective identification play a most important role. I argue in Chapter 2 that class collective action depends critically on the presence of a solidaristic culture among workers. But there is nothing in the class structure that guarantees its emergence. The sense of mutuality and shared goals needs to be forged through consciously directed agency. This suggests that culture occupies a very different place in the dynamics of class structure and class formation. The class *structure* is not constrained by the subjective identifications of its occupants, as I show in Chapter 1. But class *formation* is powerfully constrained by workers' identity and subjectivity. It is only if the arduous task of building a sense of mutual obligation is successful that the hurdles to collective action are overcome. But precisely because that work is so hard and typically ends in failure, the forging of political identities turns out to be a highly contingent outcome. And its very contingency, the high incidence of defeat and organizational breakdown of labor movements, means the most natural form of resistance will be of an individual kind.

Building on this argument, in Chapter 3 I revisit the central question of postwar social theory: given the deep antagonisms capitalism generates, how does it survive? This is perhaps where the cultural turn has been most influential. According to a very powerful line of argument, dominant classes secure their rule by establishing an *ideological hegemony*, which elicits the consent of subaltern groups. But the conclusions of Chapter 2 allow a different explanation. Cultural theorists are correct to suggest that capitalism can stabilize itself through eliciting the consent of the laboring classes. But they make two errors in this judgment. First, they are wrong to think that the source of this consent is ideological or cultural socialization. The real source is the coordination of interests between employers and employees. Second, they are mistaken in suggesting that consent is the fundamental source of stability. I argue that the latter is, in fact, secondary to another factor. The deeper, more fundamental mechanism is what I call *resignation*. Workers submit to capitalism not because they view it as legitimate or just but because they see no real possibility for changing it. Their only reasonable option therefore is to reconcile to it.

What induces workers to resign themselves to their subordination is the logic of collective action, which I describe in Chapter 2. Since a genuine challenge to the system requires successful collective action, and the latter is, in fact, highly episodic and temporary in capitalism, the typical situation is for workers to either resort to individual modes of resistance or submit to the authority of the employer—not because they are duped by ideology but because it is rational to do so. This guarantees that the baseline tendency in the system is toward stability. Now, in the event that organizations for collective action are successfully generated, the mode of integration can change from baseline resignation to one of consent. This is what happens when trade unions negotiate around the interests of their members. Workers engage in a political exchange with their employers, which is an institutionalization of consent. But this means that consent cannot be the bedrock for political stability, since institutions like unions have only been around for a part of capitalist history and only in some regions of the world. What keeps the system in place is the deeper fact of political resignation.

The first three chapters show that it is possible to have a theory of class structure and class formation that rests on recognizably "materialist" foundations. I now explore what this means for social theory more broadly. Is such a theory able to appreciate social agency? And, in the overriding concern for universal structural properties of capitalism, can it accommodate variation and contingency?

In Chapter 4, I show that, far from effacing facts about agency, a structural class theory in fact relies upon it. It assumes that, regardless of their historical or geographical location, people are able to understand their situation, successfully navigate its challenges, and act in accordance with their interests. In fact, the denial of agency is more commonly found in cultural theory, in which there has been a too frequent resort to explanations based on cognitive failure, irrationality, or ideological indoctrination. All such explanations presume agential failure, a breakdown of the requirements for social agency. Furthermore, I show that at a more macro level, the theory defended in the book so far can explain variation in the institutional forms of capitalism in the postwar era—indeed, far more successfully than a strong culturalist theory. I do so by examining the evolution of the political economies of the advanced industrial world over the recent decades. I show that a structural class theory can explain both the common patterns of development as well as the differences between them. Hence, a commitment to structural principles need not come at the expense of social agency or an attention to variation.

The final chapter brings together the elements of the arguments thus far and mobilizes them to understand the long sweep of capitalist restructuring and class formation over the past century. I offer a diagnosis of the current power balance between labor and capital by comparing it to the scene one hundred years ago, when the modern labor movement exploded onto the scene. The purpose of this chapter is to illustrate, in very broad strokes, that a materialist class theory provides a consistent, internally coherent, and empirically supported narrative about the rise and decline of the Left across the twentieth century, without the gaps and question begging that assail the culturalist attempts at the same endeavor. For if the goal is to revive the social forces that pushed toward a more humane social order, social theory will have to come back from its cultural turn.

I

Class Structure

Capitalism is an economic system that is identified with a specific class structure. While there are many social divisions within the system, as there are in any complex economy, there is one specific division taken by nearly every framework to be essential to it—the one between those who control society's productive assets and those who have none. To put it more directly, the defining characteristic of capitalism is a class structure with asset-owning capitalists on one side and a class of asset-poor workers on the other. That structure is described as fundamental to capitalism because the system's historically distinctive macro properties derive from it.

In all materialist accounts of this class structure, it is theorized as a set of social positions that assign a certain role to the people located within them. Hence, anyone described as a "capitalist" is taken to be a person in this social position, whose actions in the economy can be assumed to be directed toward specific goals. And someone designated a "wage laborer" can similarly be described as following the goals and constraints attached to that position. The economic strategies associated with the class position are taken to derive from the *position,* not the personal or cultural qualities of the person inhabiting it. Thus, an economic theory will predict that a capitalist will pursue a profit-maximizing strategy regardless of his personality and a wage laborer will seek to sell his labor power whatever his personal preferences happen to be. These are somewhat stylized assumptions, of course. In reality, there are employers who sometimes settle for a break-even approach as long as they can get away with it and wage laborers who decide to opt out of work when they can. But every economic theory of class has to insist that these cases are deviations from the norm, not the norm itself. They cannot retreat to the view that these assumptions are only convenient fictions to create elegant models if they also believe—which class theory certainly does—that they actually predict real outcomes.

Marx certainly held to the view that the behavioral assumptions of his theory captured real facts about the world—in particular, how social actors respond to structural pressures. And the foundational premise of his theory was that the class structure exerts real pressure on its incumbents so that it inclines them toward specific economic strategies. Hence, what drives the system are the causal properties of the structural positions, not the personal details of the individuals who happen to be situated in them. This is how the class structure generates the system's "laws of motion"—its macroeconomic dynamics. Locations that can be described as belonging to the same category—steel manufacturer, fast-food worker, or investment banker—induce the people located within them to pursue broadly similar economic goals, which aggregate into large-scale patterns of economic behavior.

The challenge for such a theory is to explain whether we are justified in expecting that a class structure will generate a predictable economic practice, whatever its cultural context. The reasoning behind the challenge goes something like this. All economic strategy is a species of social action. And all action, by definition, is meaning oriented. It is motivated by the particular way actors understand their situation, and those understandings are derived from the ideological and symbolic universe into which the person has been socialized. But this appears to run up against the basic assumptions of structural class theory. As we have just seen, in that theory, agents' structural locations are supposed to impel them into patterns of social action that can be predicted simply on the basis of their structural location. This suggests that the motivation stems from the structure, unmediated by the cultural and ideological socialization of the actor. And this, in turn, makes it appear that, for materialists, class processes exist outside of culture so that economic agents function on the basis of a rationality that has no connection to their identity or moral valuations. If this is so, we have to be suspicious of a theory that seems to evacuate culture from any domain of social interaction, even the economic.

The premise of the culturalist argument is undoubtedly correct. There is no structure that is free of culture and no social action that is unaffected by meaning constellations. So how is a materialist class theory, which insists on the primacy of structure over culture, even possible? In this chapter, I try to show that we can accept the premise that structures have to be interpreted by agents . . . while rejecting the conclusion, derived by many cultural theorists, that structural class theory has to be doubted, if not abandoned altogether. Materialists therefore do not have to imply that class action exists outside culture; indeed, they can affirm the latter's ubiquity in social life. With the argument vindicated, we can then move on to the other, still daunting worries about a materialist class theory, which I engage in the chapters to follow.

1.1

Culture and Social Structure

The challenge to materialist theory is ably summarized by William Sewell, one of its most influential critics in the 1990s. He recounts the early days of the cultural turn, when traditional historians like himself, trained in a kind of structural analysis, first encountered the arguments of cultural anthropology, a field that played an enormously influential part in the turn away from materialism. Whereas traditional theory was based on a prioritization of social structure as the fount of analysis, the argument from culture insisted that "the social world was constituted *by the interpretive practices* of the actors who made it up." Hence, *"even social and economic structures,* which appeared to be the concrete foundations or bony skeletons of social life, were themselves *products* of the interpretive work of human actors."[1]

But what does it mean to say that a social structure is the *product* of the "interpretive work" of social agents? It seems to designate a very powerful role to culture in the reproduction of social structures; indeed, it would seem to suggest that the latter are creations of the former. Minimally, it suggests that the agents' participation in the structure depends on first understanding and then internalizing their role in it. The structure depends on the agents' unpacking of a cultural script. Hence, the very existence of the structure seems to depend on the vagaries of cultural mediation.

This description is undoubtedly accurate for very many, even most, social structures. Consider the example of a religious congregation.

The relations that bind together the priest with his parish are a kind of structure. Its relata are the priest and the members of the church. And participation in that structure situates them relative to one another in patterned behavior. That structure will remain inert unless its relata—the people it binds together—accept their roles in it. But in order for them to accept these roles, they first have to apprehend what their participation entails. If you simply herded people into a church without their having understood and accepted the norms of comportment, it would amount to nothing more than a collection of individuals occupying a small space together. Thus, the members have to understand the difference between the roles of priest and laity; the laity has to not only apprehend the significance of the rituals but also be willing to concede to the priest his authority, both over them and over the sanctity of the practices; they have to understand how they are supposed to relate to one another within the rituals and also in the quotidian dimensions of the gatherings; the priest, in turn, has to have some mastery of the symbolic universe that supervenes on the ritual gatherings, as well as power to ordain the members of the congregation, to distinguish between the profane and the holy, and so on.

Clearly, the actors have to be socialized into their roles as a precondition for the structures being activated at all. But it is also true that as the actors struggle to understand the codes and schemas attached to the structure, they have to filter them through the cultural universe they already inhabit. They do not come to the structures as a tabula rasa. They are already acculturated to certain norms of comportment and ways of relating to the world—a particular sensibility into which they have to integrate the new codes. This is what Patrick Joyce seems to have in mind when he insists that interests cannot be derived directly from economic structures because they are "constructed through the agency of social identities."[2] They are "constructed" in that actors have to put work into the interpretive process to successfully navigate the social structure. But the tools they use in this construction are the meanings, schemas, beliefs, and sensibilities with which they are already endowed—the basis of their existing identities. Hence, structures do not just create identities, they are filtered through the identities with which the actors are already endowed.

This is the sense in which structures are activated through the construction of meaning. It clearly seems that unless the cultural processes are correctly handled, the structures will never come into being at all. They seem, therefore, to be produced by culture. Now, with this comes an important corollary—if it takes interpretive effort to acquire cultural competency in the roles attached to the structures, it stands to reason that the effort can also fail. There is an irreducible degree of contingency to the acquisition of meaning for the social actors. First of all, the actor might fail to adequately *understand* the details of the role he is expected to fill. In the case of the congregation, a member of the laity may come to the rituals with a set of expectations forged by his prior identity as a member of a different religion and may fail to adjust to the rigors of the new one; the priest, for his part, could fail to learn the intricacies of his role—the nuances of the incantations, the vast corpus of texts that comprise the religion's doctrine, or even the chain of hierarchy within the priesthood.

A second source of breakdown would be if the actor chose to *reject* the role attached to the structure. In the congregation, members might decide that the demands placed on them by the religion are too many or too exacting. Or they might find religions that are more fulfilling, that generate a sense of belonging more aligned to the actor's desires. They might even decide to turn away from religion altogether and seek solace in more worldly affairs. Either way, there is a possibility that actors might not adopt the meaning orientation required by the structure. And if this is so, the structure will break down or never acquire an anchor in the community.

So, the culturalist framework rests on two pillars:

- *The argument from meaning:* Social structures require the appropriate meaning orientation on the part of social actors.
- *The argument from contingency:* The process of meaning formation is vulnerable to breakdown and hence highly contingent.

The distinction is important because, without the argument from contingency, it is very hard to maintain the explanatory priority of culture over structure. We might agree that all structures require a certain meaning orientation from actors. But if we could just *assume* that agents *will* acquire and internalize the interpretative scheme appropriate to their structural position, the suggestion that structures depend on culture—or that they are "the *product* of the interpretive work of social actors," in Sewell's words—would lose warrant. For we could very well accept that a social structure needs actors to understand and accept the roles that come with it but also predict that once the structure is in place, the actors' role identification will simply follow in train—that is, the structure itself will induce actors to orient themselves in the needed fashion. If so, then insisting on the analytical priority of culture becomes hard to sustain because it will really be the structure that is pushing the causal process. If we are sure the implantation of the structure will itself be enough to instill actors with the appropriate meaning orientation, the key link in the chain is not culture but the antecedent structure. *Culture* would turn out to be an effect of *structure* and not vice versa, as Sewell suggests. Hence, the mere requirement of interpretive competence is not a threat to a materialist class analysis.

The real power of the culturalist framework rests on the idea that meaning not only activates structure but its availability to carry out this task might be highly variable. Culture's importance as the decisive link in the chain is elevated if it happens that the needed socialization might not materialize—if actors might not understand their roles or if they reject the required value orientation, even in the presence of structural pressures. This being the case, all the action can be taken to occur at the point of meaning construction and internalization, not at the point of the antecedent structure. Hence, the causal role of culture indeed comes to the fore. It becomes the arbiter of how actors respond to their structural location, and the latter becomes captive to the former's function and effect.

1.2
How Class Structure Is Different

The question for us is whether *class* is a structure that depends on a highly contingent cultural mediation, as I have just described it. No doubt it depends on actors' internalization of the norms appropriate to its reproduction, as do all structures. But is there a deep contingency to this internalization process so that the structure's stability cannot be taken for granted until a host of exogenous cultural factors are also present? In the following, I show that, when it comes to capitalist class relations, there is no such contingency.

The Logic of Wage Labor

Consider the situation of a wage laborer. Suppose that, much like the member of the church congregation, he approaches his new structural location with little knowledge of how it works. Perhaps he was of peasant origin and, having been recently proletarianized, is habituated into the values and expectations of a rural smallholder. Clearly, he has to undergo some kind of cultural adjustment if he is to survive as a wage laborer. He has to understand that his new vocation has a set of demands and norms that are entirely different than what he was accustomed to while working his own land; he has to decode what it means to search for work, compared to working on his own plot; he has to accept that his employer has authority over him, that he must retain his job over time, and so on. These changes are not, by any means, trivial. They require the construction of an appropriate cultural stance, an interpretive scheme that enables him to navigate his place in the structure. Hence, wage labor, no less than the church congregation, requires that actors internalize the appropriate codes—or else the structure will remain inert.

The adoption of an appropriate meaning orientation would seem to put class structures in the same state of cultural construction as the church congregation. But the priority of culture over structure needs more—the norm internalization must also be a contingent affair. So we need to ask, is there any reason to expect that this process of cultural education might fail? Recall that there are two avenues for failure—a breakdown in meaning and a refusal to participate. Now, a breakdown in meaning requires that the actor fails to *understand* the obligations of his place in the social structure. In this case, it would entail that he cannot comprehend that, having been deprived of every other source of income, he should seek out employment. Or that, having found employment, he now needs to provide his services to the person paying him. He might, of course, recoil at the idea of having to do so, and I will address that shortly. The question here is not whether he resists accepting his new situation but whether he. could fail to understand it.

I am not aware of any instance in modern history where a transition to capitalism was derailed, or even significantly delayed, by the inability of social actors to understand what wage labor *meant*. All it calls for is that the wage laborer knows that if he lacks productive assets, he must seek out those who possess them and ask for employment; the employment will have to be sought out by entering the labor market and will not come knocking at his door; he must show up for work every day if he wants to maintain the job; and he needs to follow some basic instructions while at work. The simple fact is that every premodern culture with settled agriculture already has the codes needed to assimilate to these demands. Every such culture has diverse forms of employment, and wage labor was widespread even in premodern economies; laborers have had to adjust to the authority of economic elites, so they already understand the place of domination in labor extraction, for example. None of this is a cultural conundrum. Indeed, the reason peasants have resisted proletarianization so often is precisely because they *understand all too well* what it means to be at the mercy of the labor market. They very quickly picked up its attendant loss of autonomy, the precariousness entailed by it, their inevitable subordination to their employer's profit imperative, and so on. Hence, while many social structures might impose high interpretive requirements on social actors, wage labor is not one of them.

That leaves us with a refusal to participate as the potential source of failure. Suppose the newly proletarianized worker has been raised to despise the idea of waged employment, perhaps because his culture values self-sufficiency or abhors the monetization of goods. Thus, his cultural training—the set of meanings he attaches to wage labor— inclines him to reject it altogether. What is the likelihood that he chooses to opt out, as the congregation member was free to do? It is in considering this question that the distinctiveness of class structure becomes apparent. Like all social relations, it requires the internalization of a set of codes. But class—and, in particular, wage labor—is unique in the fact that its codes relate to the actor's physical survival. To opt out is realistic only if there is an alternative means of economic support. But, in assuming he is a proletarian, we are also supposing he lacks such means—he does not have access to common land, social insurance, income from corporate stocks, or similar supports. To opt out is to deny himself his only source of income.

Now, of course, he is still formally free to walk away. It is possible, and in some instances has happened, that someone with his normative orientation is willing to risk eschewing his only source of livelihood. But such cases are pathological—extremely rare deviations from the norm. The typical reaction will be for the socialization, which imbues him with a hatred of wage labor, to lose its motivational force. For he now has to choose between holding to the norms he has cherished and experiencing a catastrophic decline in his physical well-being or accepting the loathsome necessity of waged labor. Unless he is fanatically devoted to his antecedent values, the proletarian will most likely find a way to accommodate his value system to what participation in wage labor asks of him. This does not have to take the form of an explicit, clearly articulated critique of his prior values and a wholesale rejection of his cultural training. He does not have to celebrate his new location in the structure. He simply has to adjust to it. It can just be a subtle shift in normative priorities, or the grudging acceptance of the constraint, or even an unspoken turn to the new practice left unacknowledged—never openly articulated but nevertheless followed consistently.

The proletarian's acceptance of his new role is effectuated by the economic pressure of his class position. He experiences it as a kind of *economic compulsion*.[3] In this, the forces acting upon him are quite different from most any other social relation. Consider again the parishioner discussed earlier. If he chose to refuse the role assigned to him by the church, he could very well suffer a cost. The community might impose sanctions upon him; he could face ostracism or a denial of certain social privileges; he might find that access to land is conditional on membership in the religion; he might also face physical intimidation. Indeed, many social structures are maintained by some mix of coercive mechanisms to ensure that participants do not simply "walk away."

In both structures, there is a limitation of choices for the individual. But in the case of the parishioner, the limits are maintained by some kind of *agent-imposed sanctions*. These depend on continuous monitoring by social agencies and, on top of that, willful intervention by other members of the community. It amounts to a kind of interpersonal coercion—a direct interference by other agencies in his decision-making—and is maintained through the threat or exercise of coercion. His participation is thus ensured by a socially imposed punishment, and his refusal to participate is recognized as a transgression, a breaking of convention. But whereas a recalcitrant parishioner has to be coerced by an external agency into participating, no such external intervention is necessary in the wage laborer's case. No one has to monitor him or use social pressure to keep him in the fold. He does not have to be dragged back to the workplace or be threatened by social sanctions because his deteriorating well-being is enough to make him reconsider. His economic vulnerability is enough to push him back into the social structure, should he choose to opt out. So, whereas the parishioner is *coerced* to participate, the proletarian *feels compelled* to do so simply by dint of his circumstances. To put it differently, the coercion does not have to be imposed on him by other parties; it is built into the structure of choices itself.

This is why, even though class structure requires an appropriate cultural orientation by social actors, the latter are still causally subordinate to the former. The construction of the cultural codes needed to activate it is not an exogenous, contingent process, the way it is for so many structures. Whereas there is a real possibility in other social relations that actors may fail to properly align to them, wage labor creates a powerful incentive for its practitioners to achieve competency. Indeed, the wage laborer will not only accept the new codes, he will make it his mission to learn them because to fail in this endeavor can cause a loss of livelihood. His structural location will push him to acquire the appropriate meaning orientation. Hence, culturalists are wrong to insist that class agency of the sort just described is the *effect* of the actor's meaning orientation. On the contrary, we can affirm that the proletarian's *meaning orientation* is the effect of his *structural location.*

The Logic of Being a Capitalist

Consider now the situation of the employer. Does being a capitalist also require a prior socialization into the appropriate norms, which are only sporadically and contingently available? Interestingly, there is a venerable tradition in sociology that answers in the affirmative. For close to two decades in the postwar era, many proponents of modernization theory wondered whether the newly developing countries of the Global South would be able to embark on a path of capitalist development, as Europe had before them. They were inspired by a particular reading of Max Weber's *Protestant Ethic*, which they took to be arguing that capitalism depends upon a specific meaning orientation appropriate to its economic logic.[4] For this brand of Weberian theory, the critical point is that having the right kind of value system is a *precondition* for capitalism to implant itself successfully, which makes the spread of this economic system dependent on a prior shift in culture. Hence, the worry was that Confucian, Buddhist, or Hindu religions might fail to provide the kind of normative outlook that Protestantism generated in western Europe. The market forces pushing their way into the East would thus remain stunted because merchants and businessmen would lack the entrepreneurial spirit of their counterparts in Europe.[5]

Modernization theory went into rapid decline by the late 1970s, in part because it was clear that the regions that were supposed to have suffered from the absence of a culturally induced entrepreneurial spirit were developing not only very rapidly but at rates the world had never seen. Japan, Korea, Taiwan, and even India were experiencing economic growth orders of magnitude greater than any European country had during the first two industrial revolutions. What is more, their rates of private investment reached heights that had been thought unattainable just two decades prior. Where was the motivation for this investment coming from, in such diverse cultures, across so many regions, if their economic actors lacked the appropriate cultural orientation for it? If there was a specific "spirit" that had to be internalized by capitalists as a precondition to their success, it was clear that it was pretty widely available.

The alternative explanation for the spread of capitalist investment patterns is that it does not depend on prior implantation of an entrepreneurial spirit at all. Rather, it creates the needed outlook endogenously through the pressure exerted on capitalists by their structural location. A capitalist is someone who not only employs wage labor but has to compete on the market to sell his product. He is thus market dependent in two ways—in having to purchase his inputs, as opposed to generating them himself, and in having to bring in enough revenue from sales to keep his operation afloat. The viability of his undertaking depends on outcompeting his rivals in the market. The only effective way of achieving this in the long run is by finding ways to reduce his selling prices *without* cutting into his profit margins. This requires him to find ways of increasing his efficiency, hence reducing his unit costs and thereby preserving his margins even as he slashes the selling price or, conversely, maintaining his selling price while improving the quality of the product. But neither of these is possible in the long run without substantial investments in better inputs—better capital goods, skills, materials, and so on, which requires that he choose, on his own volition, to prioritize investing his earnings rather than consuming them. If he dissipates his earnings on personal consumption, he will, of course, increase his pleasure temporarily, but at the cost of undermining his viability as a capitalist. Simply surviving the competitive battle thus forces capitalist to prioritize the qualities associated with the "entrepreneurial spirit."

Hence, the pressure emanating from the capitalist's structural location exercises its own discipline on him—whether he is Hindu, Muslim, Confucian, or Protestant. Whatever his prior socialization, he quickly learns that he will have to conform to the rules attached to his location or his establishment will be driven under. It is a remarkable property of the modern class structure that any significant deviation by a capitalist from the logic of market competitiveness shows up as a cost in some way—a refusal to dump toxic sludge manifests as a loss in market share to those who will; a commitment to use safer but more expensive inputs shows up as a rise in unit costs, and so on. Capitalists thus feel an enormous pressure to *adjust* their normative orientation—their values, goals, ethics, and so on—to the social structure in which they are embedded, not vice versa, as with so many other social relations. The moral codes that are encouraged are those that help the bottom line. Sometimes this can be consistent with a nonmarket morality—as, for example, when offering to pay high wages just out of decency has the result of raising productivity. But the point is that the market tells the capitalist which elements of his moral universe are viable and which are not—rather than vice versa.

Of course, there will be many who fail to conform. In these cases, the enterprises they supervise or own will slowly lose competitiveness and will ultimately cease to be viable. But this, in turn, has two effects that only harden the tendency toward cultural adjustment— first, there will be a demonstration effect for other economic actors, both existing and potential capitalists, who will note that the refusal to abandon outmoded values caused the failure; second, it will reduce the proportion of the entrepreneurs who hold to the latter sort of beliefs and hence dilute their influence on the culture. There will therefore be a kind of selection process that winnows away those normative orientations that clash with the rules required of capitalist reproduction. So even though there will always be those who refuse, or are unable, to adjust their moral universe to the requirements of being a capitalist, the market itself ensures they will remain on the fringes of the economic system.

Again, much as the case with wage labor, we see that the meaning orientation of the capitalist is causally relevant to the action, but this orientation is the effect of the structure, rather than the other way around. The actor's class location impels him to adopt a stance consistent with the structure's demands, and if he fails in this regard, the market selects against him—it drives him out and replaces him with someone more culturally competent. The aggregate effect is for a culture to develop around this practice that condones and advances the latter.

1.3

Two Models of Cultural Influence

The preceding discussion revealed that it is possible to accept that structures depend on meaning acquisition while denying to the latter an *explanatory primacy* over structure. To say that structures depend on culture is to assign the latter a specific sort of causal role. It intervenes between the structure and social action and, in so doing, connects them by virtue of its intervention. Culturalists and materialists can both agree on this. Where they differ is not on how culture relates to *action* but on how it relates to the antecedent *structure*. In the culturalist argument, the causal influence of the structure on the process of meaning construction is very weak, even nonexistent. In other words, the structure itself does not generate the appropriate constellation of meaning. This is why the construction of the appropriate meaning constellations cannot be taken for granted and why the generation of the appropriate social action is also highly contingent. The causal logic of this argument is diagrammed in Model 1 (see Figure 1.1).

In this model, culture is presented as a causal mechanism that *mediates* the relation between structure and action. Mediating mechanisms intervene between a cause and an effect, but they are exogenous

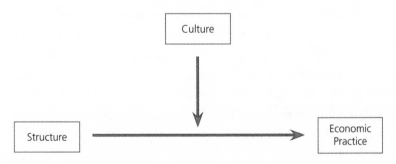

Figure 1.1 Model 1: Intervention as Causal Mediation

38

to the chain that connects the former to the latter.[6] In the diagram, the exogeneity is captured in the fact that there is no arrow connecting the structure to this mechanism. It is brought about by processes independent of that particular social structure. Its availability cannot therefore be predicted by the mere presence of the structure. This carries two implications. First, the probability of the outcome cannot be predicted until we know the likelihood of the mediating cause's availability. Second, the nature of the outcome also substantially rests on the properties of the mediating cause. Whether or not the outcome occurs, as well as the various properties of the outcome, cannot be predicted simply by knowing the facts about the antecedent cause. It will depend on the presence, and the character, of the mediating mechanism. This lends it an enormous, independent role in the outcome's explanation.

The case of the parish is meant to illustrate this principle. Culture here plays the role of a mediating mechanism; not only is it the proximate cause of the structure's survival, but its operation cannot be taken for granted. Actors might reject the roles they are assigned and walk away or might somehow fail to understand them. To implant them with the appropriate meaning orientation requires a certain level of external intervention, and it is the efficacy of this intervention that mediates the relation between the actor and the structure. Because that efficacy cannot be taken for granted—and might, in fact, fail—it heightens the explanatory role of culture in the structure's reproduction.

This is not the case with wage labor or capital. Here, culture is still the proximate cause of the structure's stability in that it provides the codes and meanings needed to activate the structures—much as with the example of the parish. But it does not play the role of a mediating mechanism because its efficacy is not nearly so contingent as in the other case. It does not independently shape the outcome so much as *it* is shaped by the *antecedent* cause. This turns it more into a *transmission* channel for the latter's influence. In this case, we have the structure *shaping* the cultural codes that orient the actor in the appropriate way. This is presented in Model 2 of causal intervention (see Figure 1.2).

Model 2 also requires that the proximate cause of a structure's activation is culture. Where it differs is that it radically reduces the contingency of that process. The structure itself places limits on the variation in cultural codes. The curved arrows denote a causal feed-back loop that establishes the compatibility of the agents' meaning orientation with the class structure. The arrow going right to left is dotted because the interaction between structure and culture is not symmetrical: the influence of the former is more powerful than of the latter, as expressed in the density of the arrows from one to the other.[7] Thus, if the actor's values or norms are out of sync with what is required of the structure, he will find good reason to revise those norms *without external intervention.*

Whereas the congregation member can refuse the norms required of the church, this option is not typically available to wage laborers or capitalists. A worker will find good reason to either rapidly adjust her initially negative valuation of wage labor or just take the latter on, however grudgingly—for to refuse to do so will be to imperil her own survival. The owner of a firm will also adjust his practice regardless of his moral commitments—for to refuse is to endanger

Figure 1.2 Model 2: Intervention as Causal Transmission

the firm's viability. Just as importantly, in the event that the actors do not, in fact, adjust their norms, the structure will simply weed them out—they will not survive.[8] Over time, the broad pattern of norms that govern the structure will evolve in a relation of compatibility with its demands, either via actors adjusting their values to the structure or by recalcitrant actors being weeded out. Hence, even though the proximate cause for the structure's activation is still culture, the structure itself ensures the appropriate codes will be available.

1.4

The Causal Autonomy of Class Structure

The preceding discussion has established the fundamental premise of materialism—that class structure works *through* culture but is not *constrained* by it. On the contrary, economic actors' meaning orientation is constrained to adjust to the demands of the structure. If this is so, it means the structure's causal influence is established *independently* of the facts pertaining to local codes and mores. In other words, the class structure cannot be derailed by the vagaries of the local meaning constellations. If they are out of sync with the demands of the structure, the actors will take it upon themselves to adopt new ones. This effectively reverses the culturalist argument. Whereas culture has explanatory priority over structure in the latter, it turns out that in the case of class, structure enjoys an explanatory priority over culture. This formulation enables us to address two issues that have been central to the debate on culture and interests over the past decades.

Economy and Culture—Separate and Unequal?

Any talk of economic structures enjoying some kind of autonomy from culture is often viewed with great skepticism by social theorists, including many Marxists. The formulation seems to suggest that causal independence denotes a social separation, that economic action is somehow separate from culture, values, morals, and so on. There can be no doubt that there is a powerful semantic footprint in Marxian theory that treats class structure as separate from the cultural domain. The language of many early Marxists—and, indeed, even theorists of postwar vintage—is imbued with this image, as when theorists wonder if something is "in the superstructure" or "in the base," as if they are a collection of storage rooms; or in Louis Althusser's talk of the cultural and economic "levels," as if they were stacked one upon the other; and, of course, Engels's famous allowance that sometimes the superstructure can also act upon the base, which seems to suggest an institutional separation between the two. It is easy to see how a materialism expressed thusly seems impossible to defend. One of its most fulsome rejections came from E. P. Thompson in his debate with Althusser. Taking the example of legal institutions, Thompson lampooned the idea that they were housed comfortably in the superstructure or, in Althusser's language, comprised a different "level" than the economy. "I found," he declared, "that law did not keep politely to a 'level' but was at *every* bloody level." The rest of his admonishment is worth quoting, if only for its rhetorical brilliance:

> It [the law] was imbricated within the mode of production and productive relations themselves (as property-rights, definitions of agrarian practice) and it was simultaneously present in the philosophy of Locke; it intruded brusquely within alien categories, reappearing bewigged and gowned in the guise of ideology; it danced a cotillon with religion, moralising over the theatre of Tyburn; it was an arm of politics and politics was one of its arms; it was an academic discipline, subjected to

the rigour of its own autonomous logic; it contributed to the definition of the self-identity both of rulers and of ruled; above all, it afforded an arena for class struggle, within which alternative notions of law were fought out.[9]

Even though Thompson's diatribe was focused on the law, he would have been equally adamant that culture, too, was to be found "at every bloody level." It is the very idea of separating economic relations from the other dimensions of social life that he, like many other theorists, rejected.

It should be plain enough that the argument I am defending presumes no such separation of economic and cultural domains. In the class theory I defend, economic activity is no less steeped in culture than is any other social practice. This is what it means to affirm, as I do, that the proximate trigger for social action is the meaning orientation of the actor—his values, morality, desires, and so on. These do not subsist in a separate compartment in his life. A worker, for example, does not deposit them in a room before he comes to work and pick them up on his way home. They are operative in his economic activity no less than they are in his life away from work. His participation in all the social relations he inhabits is activated through culture.

What a materialist class theory claims is not that culture is *absent* in economic activity but that its content *adjusts* to accommodate the economic. The challenge is to provide a mechanism that explains how and why such an adjustment might come about, without having to resort to functionalist arguments. The mechanism here is plainly in the intentionality of social action. Actors inserted into wage labor or capital ownership positions seek to reproduce themselves as best they can. In this, they mobilize their views and valuations of their situation. These values are either compatible with a successful strategy of economic reproduction or come into tension with it. And if the latter, actors perceive them as a hindrance to their reproduction. And when they do come into conflict thus, the actors find good reason to adjust them so their economic viability is not threatened. Either way, they are always acting through, and within, some particular meaning orientation. They are always steeped in culture.

We can affirm, then, that material reproduction and meaning construction are two dimensions of the *same* activity, not two different *kinds* of activity. Hence, to suggest that one is independent of the other cannot denote a social separation of the two. What it describes is a causal subordination of one part of the duo to the other. It suggests that even though the two are always implicated in the reproduction of class structure, their interaction is asymmetrical, the one placing limits on the operation of the other. Thompson's worries about materialism turn out to be misplaced, even while his excoriation of Althusser's version of materialism is laudable.

A Global Engine

A second implication of my argument for class structure's causal autonomy is that it allows us to explain the global spread of capitalism. The most important implication of a materialist class theory is that there is a determinate relation between the structure and social action, whatever the content of the local culture. Class structure operates by dramatically narrowing the range of reasonable options for economic actors, and, in so doing, it elicits a broadly similar kind of response from the latter. And these broadly similar responses at the *micro* level aggregate into *macro*-level social patterns. This property of the structure explains how capitalist economies exhibit broadly similar dynamics in regions that are so divergent in their history, religion, and norms.

On the other hand, the inability to explain this simple social fact is the biggest weakness of culturalism. Any theory that rests its case on locality and contingency, as culturalism does, faces an uphill task when confronted with the indubitable fact of capitalism's expansion across the globe and the obvious similarity in its macrodynamics across these regions. Culturalists either have to illicitly import materialist assumptions into their historical narratives or, when operating at a more conceptual level, are forced to deny the regularities the system undeniably exhibits. What is easily explicable with a materialist theory looms as an uncomfortable anomaly for its culturalist alternative. This very discomfort has created something of an intellectual crisis over the past decade, and any attempt to rescue the theory must honestly confront it.

Of course, the case for materialist class theory still needs a great deal more. This chapter has only set the foundations for a fuller explication of its elements, not just on the matter of structure but also for the critical problem of class formation and, ultimately, for the deepest puzzle of all—the balance between conflict and stability in capitalism. On a more metatheoretical level, I still have to more fully address what it means for structures to reduce the contingency in actors' responses. Just how binding are the constraints on social action? How much room is there for contingency? The theory stresses a convergence in macrodynamics, but can it also accommodate the variations among those patterns? These are the issues addressed in the rest of the book. The burden of this chapter has been to lay the foundation for such questions.

2

Class Formation

In classical Marxism, the capitalist class structure has two fundamental causal properties: one economic and the other political. Economically, throwing all productive establishments onto the market forces them into a competitive battle as a means of survival. Only those firms survive that can outcompete their rivals in the marketplace. This compels them to adopt a strategy of reducing unit costs to sell at lower prices without eating into their margins, thereby driving their rivals out of the market and securing their own position. This *cost-minimizing* strategy is just the flip side of *profit maximization.* Now, most economic theories, classical and neoclassical, recognize that *micro*-level profit maximization is the foundation for many of the *macro*-level phenomena characteristic of capitalist economies— the business cycle, periodic recessions, banking crises, the unemployment level, and so on. These economy-wide phenomena are the unintended consequences of millions of individual firms trying to maximize profits—individually rational, but making for a very unstable macroeconomy.

This very process of economic reproduction is also supposed to generate a political consequence—the organization of workers into a class that then takes on the class of employers. Classical Marxists considered this process, which we shall refer to as *class formation*, to be a consequence of the class structure itself. They thought there were facts about the class structure that created a powerful impulse for workers to come together as a class; hence, class formation was a *consequence* of the class structure. This does not mean they took it as inevitable, even if, in some of his rhetorical flourishes, Marx certainly gave the impression that he did. But they did think there were pressures emanating from the class structure itself that both motivated and enabled workers to organize themselves. The workers' location within the class structure would generate a consciousness of their common interests with their peers, which, in turn, would induce them to forge organizations to fight for those interests and then eventually topple the system.

The expectation that workers will overthrow the system, as capitalism's "gravediggers," has obviously been frustrated. But suppose we weaken the claim so it does not predict that workers will organize to overthrow capitalism but merely that they will organize themselves *within* capitalism to defend their interests. Even this does not seem to offer much comfort. Labor's organization is at best uneven across the world; it is only in the richer countries of the West that a significant proportion of the working class has ever been unionized. The vast majority of workers in the Global South are, and always have been, unorganized; even in the North, union density has been declining for several decades such that the modal worker increasingly stands alone against his employer. Hence, even the weaker claim seems dubious. Far from being driven to band together with other members of his class, the worker seems just as likely to go it alone.

So if a theory of class formation is to have any purchase, it is obliged to jettison the apparent teleology expressed by the classical tradition. One avenue taken by most of the theory's critics is to locate the flaw in the description of the class structure—perhaps in the suggestion that it generates an antagonism between employer and employee, in the central place given to interests in the account of political agency, or even in the very idea that structures have a reality of their own. If any of these criticisms are accepted, then of course the causal connection between structure and action breaks down—and the very idea of a deterministic relation between class structure and class formation goes with it.

My argument takes a rather different turn. I suggest that the basic description of the class structure is correct—as argued in the preceding chapter. The theory's weakness resides not in the account of the class structure but in the construal of its consequences. In other words, classical Marxists derived the wrong conclusions from their understanding of the capitalist class structure. In their view, workers' location in the structure would incline them toward collective modes of defense; I argue, on the contrary, that those very same structures induce workers to prefer individual modes of resistance over collective ones. Individual contestation is therefore the norm and collective action the deviation from it. The burden of this chapter is to explain why this should be the case. But if this is so, we are left with a startling conclusion—that the same facts about the class structure that many early Marxists thought would lead to class struggle in fact militate against it. The class structure locks its incumbents into conflict, and it does so in a way that limits the latter's explosiveness. Hence, the contingency of class formation is not an anomaly but a predicted consequence of the theory. This has profound implications for the theory of hegemony and capitalist stability, which I engage in Chapter 4.

2.1

Why Should Workers Resist?

Of all the criticisms of structural class theory, the most well-known indicts it for an excessively deterministic view of class formation. Critics take the theory to predict that the class structure will necessarily generate a very specific set of interests; workers, being rational, are expected to pursue those interests collectively by waging class struggle. Structure is therefore endowed with a causal power to generate both an awareness of class interests and a desire to pursue them collectively. In other words, according to materialist class theory, especially of the Marxian variant, once a class structure is in place, it is also expected to generate a particular set of *subjective identities*—belonging to a certain class and wishing to pursue a political agenda prioritizing that identity. But—the criticism goes—this is arbitrary. Social actors have many identities, and there is no justification for expecting that actors will identify with their class experiences, instead of any of their other myriad social roles. Structural class theory works with the expectation that the experience of wage labor necessarily leads to class consciousness, and, if found not to, the case being studied is consigned to the status of "deviant," an aberration. But it turns out that the entire world deviates from the prediction of the theory. At some point, the argument goes, we have to accept that the flaw is in the theory, not the world.[1]

This worry about determinism or teleology is surely warranted. Any acceptable class theory has to acknowledge that within the

49

modern class structure, workers' identification with their class is more likely the exception, not the rule, and therefore the absence of class consciousness is not a deviation from the norm but rather is the norm. A viable class theory therefore has to provide mechanisms that account for this fact, not in an ad hoc fashion but as normal consequences of a capitalist economic structure. It then has to explain how and why, in certain conditions, a class identity can be forged.

The first challenge is to explain why workers might object to their situation at all. I argued in the preceding chapter that workers seek out employment because it is in their interests to do so. It is the only way they can sustain themselves after having been proletarianized. This means they benefit from the employment contract—or, to put it differently, they enjoy "gains from trade," much the same as the employer does. Why, then, should we expect any recalcitrance from one side of the employment contract if they are benefiting from it? It is easy to conclude, as many libertarians do, that it is an irrational response or, even more, an instance of rent seeking. An explanation of the modalities of economic conflict needs to make clear why it happens in the first place.

The Dual Character of the Employment Contract

There are two facts about the employment relation that profoundly shape all its other dynamics. The first concerns the asymmetrical relation between employer and employee. As I argued in the previous chapter, the economic circumstances of the worker *compel* him to enter the labor market in search of a job. Typically, workers do not have alternative streams of income or the savings to sustain them during long bouts of unemployment. This is in contrast to the employer, who will not only be in possession of both but, precisely because of his greater wealth, will also be favorably positioned to acquire credit if his finances run short. Even though this fact is often glossed over by neoclassical economists, it was not lost on their forebearers. As Adam Smith famously observed in *The Wealth of Nations,* whenever there is a dispute between employer and employee around wages or work conditions,

> It is not . . . difficult to foresee which of the two parties must, upon all ordinary occasions, have the advantage in the dispute, and force the other into a compliance with their terms. . . . In all such disputes the masters can hold out much longer. A landlord, a farmer, a master manufacturer, or merchant, though they did not employ a single workman, could generally live a year or two upon the stocks which they have already acquired. Many workmen could not subsist a week, few could subsist a month, and scarce any a year without employment. In the long-run the workman may be as necessary to his master as his master is to him, but the necessity is not so immediate.[2]

The inequality in assets thus translates into an inequality in bargaining power. Employers are positioned to set the basic terms of the contract, rather than it being a bargain struck between two equal parties. This is especially significant in two domains—the distribution of the firm's revenues and the internal organization of the workplace (the pace of work, its duration, the division of labor, and so on). Of course, the employee is free to reject the terms on which the job is offered or negotiate for their improvement. But precisely because of the power imbalance between the two parties, he always does so from a position of weakness. Even in cases where the employee is highly skilled or especially valued, he is able to mitigate his disadvantage but never overturn it.

Employers set the basic conditions of employment. How they shape it, the ends to which it is directed, is profoundly influenced by the second critical fact, which is that capitalists have to function under a *competitive constraint.* Survival in the market requires not just that they attract consumers to their product but that they do so against the challenge posed by rival producers. And since consumers have to operate under their own budget constraints, they will gravitate to the product sold at the lower price—controlling, of course, for quality. Hence, a primary route to market success is for firms to find ways of reducing their costs so the product can be offered at a lower price without eating into their profit margins. The direct and most common response to market competition is for the capitalist to adopt a cost-minimizing strategy. Managers are constrained to utilize their inputs as efficiently as possible, which means they try to acquire the most productive inputs at the lowest price available.

Bringing together these two facts about the employment relation, the capitalist has the authority to set the terms of employment, and market competition forces him to do it in service of a cost-minimizing strategy. In the rest of this section, we examine how this situation systematically generates antagonism between the two classes, even while their interdependence remains intact.

The Distribution of the Product

The labor contract typically has a static and a dynamic dimension. Statically, the worker and the employer agree to a particular level of remuneration, whether measured in units of time (as in wage contracts) or in product (as with piece rates). The laborer is assured that he will be remunerated at this wage as long as he is in good standing at the workplace. This is a kind of static dimension of the bargain in that the maintenance of this level of remuneration is simply the original agreement reproduced unaltered over time. The original agreement is crafted in view of the firm's economic condition at that moment, which includes its place in the market, its productivity level, and, above all, the division of its revenue between the two parties. This is the level the employer views as consistent with his profit-maximizing strategy and the laborer takes as the best he can manage in the given labor market conditions.

But, over time, as the firm's position in the market changes, it also changes the scope for the distribution of its revenue and, by extension, the orientation of the two parties toward the original contract. This is its dynamic element. In particular, as the firm ratchets up its productivity in order to compete more effectively and increase its profit stream, it opens up the possibility for income gains on both ends of the employment relation. For workers, the problem is that there is no mechanism to ensure that productivity gains will translate into higher wages. This is entirely in the hands of the employer. He decides whether the new revenue will be used for increased wages, distributed as dividends, or reinvested in new equipment. Indeed, the incentive for him is to hold the line on wages as part of his cost-minimizing imperative. The most rational strategy is to direct the wage flow into channels that will further improve his market position or perhaps toward the shareholders who have invested in the firm to maintain its status with them. Hence, there is no reason to assume that productivity gains will redound to the financial benefit of the employee; therefore, over time, he will be compelled to revisit the terms of his original agreement in order to demand an acceptable portion of the new revenues, which he will rightly claim are due at least in part to his own labor.

Now, since his employer has good reason to resist his demand for a portion of the new revenue, whether or not the employee can, in fact, capture some of the increased revenues will depend entirely on his bargaining position. His original agreement reflected his position relative to the employer at the time; what he can extract at some point in the future will depend on where he stands at that future point. It is even possible that, if his position has deteriorated, the original agreement can be revised downward by his employer. This means that income distribution is bound up with power dynamics at every stage of the employment relation—at the moment when the two parties come to an agreement and at every point subsequent to it. But this is just another way of saying that an element of conflict is built into the distribution of income between labor and capital.

The Effort Bargain

A second front on which conflict arises is on the question of the content and pace of work. As labor economists have come to understand, employers face a fundamental challenge when they pay workers for their labor power. With most other commodities, the buyer can enumerate the characteristics of the good he is set to acquire: those qualities of it that generate utility for him, the quality and quantity of which he can describe to the seller. So, in the purchase of something like fruit, he can specify which kind he wants, insist that it be in a certain quantity, demand that its quality be up to a particular level, and so on; once a physical good has been purchased, the interaction between the two parties will typically come to an end. Its consumption is remote from its point of purchase.

The purchase of labor power differs from other exchanges in important ways. Most crucially, the quality and quantity of "labor units" the workers sell to the capitalist cannot be fully specified as they can with other goods. What he sells is his services over units of *time*—whose particulars cannot be fully set out in advance. While the employer agrees to pay the worker for his labor over eight hours, it is only with a vague injunction to deliver it as directed. But how hard, fast, or careful the delivery will be—the quality and quantity of the labor units—cannot be fully enumerated because there are too many imponderables in the actual work process. Employers have to constantly adjust the pace and intensity of work as market conditions change; they have to redirect labor in accordance with changing exigencies and as they discover the actual abilities of individual workers, and so on. The agreement between the two parties is thus described as an incomplete contract.[3]

Now, incomplete contracts are not, by nature, conflictual. In many cases, the aspects left unspecified are not cause for concern because both parties want to maintain good relations and have reason to trust each other. They fill in the gaps, as it were, to the best of their ability because each stands to gain from aligning with the other's goals. But with the labor contract, the zone for mutual benefit is much narrower. For the employer, it is not enough to simply bring together a number of workers and then leave it to them to work as hard and as carefully as they see fit. He operates his establishment under a severe competitive constraint, which means that, as with all his other inputs, he has to ensure that he acquires the maximal value from his purchase. Hence, he cannot simply offer the worker a wage for the work effort that the latter deems appropriate; the employer is constrained to extract the maximal quantum of effort from the labor he has acquired. It is in his interest to ensure that his employees work as hard and as carefully as possible. For every dollar he spends on the wage, he seeks to fill up each hour with the maximal units of his employees' labor, controlling for quality. With the increased effort comes increased throughput, and as throughput increases, it drives down the unit cost of the good, enabling the capitalist to sell at lower prices without incurring losses.

This is an unqualified gain for the employer. But for the employee, it often comes at a cost. The effort level is set by the employer in service of profit maximization, not the needs of the workers. Hence, while the employer gains from ratcheting up the workload or increasing the throughput, the effect on workers might very well be an increase in injuries, more stress, physical fatigue, and the like. Higher profits for the firm are often acquired at the expense of greater physical and psychological harm incurred by its employees. What appears as an unambiguous good for the owner is at best a mixed bag for his workers and more typically induces considerable harm.

Now, if there were a mechanism to guarantee an equitable division of the additional revenue from the increased productivity between employer and employee, there would be more reason for workers to cooperate. They could regard the new pace of work as a tolerable burden because, even while it caused some suffering, they would be compensated for it with higher wages. But, of course, as we observed in the previous discussion, this is precisely what they cannot take for granted. The power over the distribution of the gains resides with the capitalist, and he has very good reason to direct it into other channels. The *costs* of an increased workload are borne more by the employee while the *gains* emanating from it flow more to the employer.

Hence, the worker has good reason to push back, to try his best to adjust the pace of work to his own needs and limits, rather than to the employer's drive for profit maximization. There are many ways for employees to resist the intensification of work. Perhaps the most well-known is "soldiering" or "shirking"—to slow down its pace, either individually or through cooperation. But perhaps most common is the simple resort to absenteeism.[4] Labor economists have observed for decades that the industries with the most demanding work conditions are also the ones with the highest rate of absenteeism and employee turnover. Some part of this is no doubt caused by the human body simply breaking down from the demands made upon it. But a substantial portion comes from a *refusal* to submit to it—a desperate attempt to reduce the wear and tear by scaling back the hours at work as long as it does not result in termination. On other occasions, employees might engage in sabotage to slow down the pace of work or even coerce one another to maintain an acceptable level of intensity.

The two parties thus continually pull in opposite directions. Employers are motivated by market pressures to maximize the labor inputs extracted from their workers, whatever the reigning technological conditions. For them, this is just a natural extension of the cost-minimizing principle. But whereas this is a desirable outcome for employers, it comes attached to real costs for employees, since they are not assured a portion of the additional revenue and the increased effort often means added physical and mental strain. The effort bargain turns into a second zone of conflict.

Insecurity

One might legitimately wonder why insecurity is listed here as a source of contention when it is a defining characteristic of the class position itself. To be a worker means to lack access to the means of production, which is just to say that being a worker means to lack economic security. In the present discussion, we are supposed to be examining negotiable aspects of the employment relation, not what it means to be a worker. Hence, a discussion of the subject would seem to be a category mistake.

While this concern has some merit, I think it is possible to consider insecurity as an attribute of the job, and not just of the worker's structural position. In other words, it is part of the terms of employment and not just a background condition for the pursuit of employment. A worker can achieve employed status with variable degrees of security. One end can provide promises of lifetime tenure while the other may entail nothing but short-term gigs with no protection at all. Because of its variable character, it cannot be taken for granted and hence will be an outcome of a bargaining process, much the same as the other two factors we have considered.

One reason to treat insecurity as an attribute of the job is that it seems to have an independent impact on employee well-being. One of the most striking findings among medical researchers is that the physical and psychological damage wrought by the fear of unemployment can even be greater than the effects of unemployment itself.[5] Of course, it also functions through its interaction with other factors. Most crucially, the degree of insecurity affects the bargaining outcomes on the other two issues—income distribution and work effort. Employees who are more vulnerable to layoffs are also more likely to accept more demanding work schedules and less generous remuneration. Hence, the rules and expectations regarding tenure become one of the issues negotiated by the two sides. For the worker, reducing his vulnerability to being sacked is not only a means for more success on the other fronts but an end valued in itself.

2.2

From Universal Antagonism to Universal Resistance

These three issues do not exhaust the zones of conflict in the employment relation. But they are probably the most enduring. Their salience derives from the fact that they are not caused by imperfections in the market or contingencies of place, culture, psychology, or personality but are built into the very nature of waged labor in capitalism. They emanate from the basic and ineradicable dilemma workers face, which is that the very same job that enables them to survive also becomes a source of considerable harm. They seek out employment in order to defend their basic well-being, but once they acquire the job, it delivers on the promise only partially or opens up entirely new fronts that threaten their well-being. The job is therefore a lifeline as well as a threat.

The Universality of Resistance

The antagonistic nature of the employment relation is something capitalism carries with it as it traverses the globe, and it binds the two classes in conflict wherever it goes. It accompanies capitalism wherever the system takes root because its drivers are not specific to any particular culture or local meanings. In the previous chapter, we observed that neither the motivation to enter the labor market nor the drive to maximize profits requires a deep prior socialization in Western or any other mores. The preceding discussion has suggested that the contested nature of work is also unmoored from any particular culture. The same material motives that push the worker to accept a job also induce him to contest the terms on which it is carried out. He agrees to it to secure his well-being; he fights over its terms because the job also undermines that very well-being. Hence, the explanation for workers resisting employers' demands does not have to make any far-reaching assumptions about their psychology or preferences. The same motivations that explain their willingness to *seek* employment can also explain their struggles once they *accept* it.

This is a crucially important fact because it suggests that, just as capitalism has a universal tendency to impose its demands on economic actors, so, too, the tendency to resist their subordination to it will also be universal.[6] It enables a materialist class theory to explain what is surely something of a puzzle for the more stridently culturalist theories: not only how capitalism imposes its compulsions in such diverse settings but also how the resistance to it has been consistent across those settings. Indeed, not just the *fact* of resistance, but the actual *demands* of the labor movement, have also tended to be quite consistent, whether in the West or the East, in colonial or postcolonial settings, or among Christians or Muslims. Any viable class theory has to be able to explain these striking patterns, which seems especially challenging for culturalist approaches to class analysis. On the other hand, one of the virtues of a materialist theory of class is that the cross-cultural facts about capitalism's spread and the contestation that has followed not only pose no threat to it but can be derived from it naturally. Marx and his early followers were therefore justified in arguing that capitalism is not only linked to a particular class structure but that the structure generates an antagonism between the classes, regardless of region or culture.

The Error of Classical Marxism

Early Marxists were less justified in their confidence that the antagonism would lead to a particular *kind* of resistance from workers—encompassing organizations dedicated to advancing their collective interests—making the transition, in Marx's words, from being a class *in* itself to becoming a class *for* itself. The argument is often explicated in a kind of teleology. But it needn't be. It is possible to reformulate it as a reasonable causal theory that describes how dimensions of workers' structural location make collective action not only rational but also likely. First, capitalism itself partially organizes workers as it brings them into the same workplace. If we compare their situation with that of smallholding peasants, it is clear that the experience of repeated interaction in enclosed spaces for long periods of time lowers the costs of some critical inputs into collective action—communication, information exchange, planning, and so forth. Second, in coming together, workers recognize their common situation. They see that they are all subject to broadly similar constraints and operate under the same structures of authority and suffer the same liabilities. Third, in this constant interaction, they create a common identity and hence a willingness to engage in common pursuits.

While Marx's argument can be presented in an acceptable causal form, the criticisms leveled at it are compelling. In some instances, workers have come together in a fashion consistent with his prediction, but there have been very long stretches in its history where we observe the opposite—not *conflict* but *stability*. Workers have shown an inclination to forge organizations for collective struggle, but this can hardly be viewed as a typical occurrence in capitalism. An equally likely situation is one in which efforts at class association are tried and fail or are avoided altogether. Widespread membership in trade unions is a recent phenomenon in capitalist history and is largely confined to only a part of the global working class.

Hence, the most we can say in favor of Marx's prediction is that it describes *one* possible outcome generated by the modern class structure. In the absence of an account of the mechanisms that undermine this causal sequence, it is easy to see why the theory can morph into a kind of teleology or at least an unjustifiably deterministic one—workers' structural location is deemed, in such accounts, to be sufficient in itself to trigger the formation of a class identity, which then impels them to create organizations around this identity and finally to forge ahead in pursuit of their common interests.

The challenge for a materialist theory is to show how, although it might be possible, under certain circumstances, for workers' antagonism with their employers to incline them to converge around a strategy of collective resistance, it is just as likely to motivate them to adopt a more individualistic one. Class consciousness, and the forms of contestation attached to it, can then be understood as a product of some very particular conditions that might have to be produced and sustained, rather than assumed to fall into place through the internal logic of the class structure. The absence of class consciousness among workers, and the sporadic or evanescent eruption of class conflict, can then be seen as being entirely consistent with a class analysis of capitalism rather than an indication of the declining salience of class.

2.3

Two Strategies of Resistance

The key to the puzzle of class formation is that optimistic prognostications like Marx's, even when they are presented in a defensible causal language, skip a crucial step. They focus on the causal mechanisms that might incline workers toward class organization but fail to describe other aspects of the class structure that mitigate *against* this course of action. As it happens, a critical property of capitalist class structure is that it positions workers in such a way that they will typically find an individualized course of class reproduction more feasible than one reliant on collective organization. Two broad kinds of obstacles play this role. The first is workers' baseline vulnerability against the power of employers, and the other is the generic problems that arise in collective action.

Workers' Vulnerability

As noted in Section 2.1, workers and their employers do not engage in political contestation in a neutral setting. They come together in a preexisting field of power in which the employer wields enormous leverage over the worker. In a landmark essay published in 1980, Claus Offe and Helmut Wiesenthal argued that the asymmetries located in the class structure extend far into the process of class formation as well.[7] Workers operate in a condition of generalized insecurity. Since they do not own productive assets of their own, they depend on waged employment under a capitalist. This dependence on their employer decisively shapes their inclination toward, and capacity for, collective action. Workers understand that they are able to hold on to their jobs only so long as it is desired by the capitalist, who can, for any variety of reasons, decide to throw one or many of them back into the labor market. The precariousness of employment is a baseline condition built into the position of being a worker, though, of course, its intensity will vary depending on how difficult it is to replace any particular employee. Hence, even though employers do not have direct legal or cultural authority over the life of any particular laborer, as is the case in slavery or serfdom, they still wield enormous indirect power over the latter.

This has a direct bearing on the likelihood of collective action. Workers typically have to prioritize the security of their employment over their inclination to struggle over the terms of that employment—in other words, they realize that having a badly paying or dangerous job is preferable to not having a job at all. But if workers' priority is to hold on to their jobs, it can only mean that they consciously forswear activities that would invite retaliation from the boss. In fact, if the employees are not already organized, the most appealing means of increasing one's job security is not taking on the boss but making oneself more attractive to him—by working harder than the others, acquiring new skills, even offering to work for less.

In a situation of generalized labor market competition, the easier means for increasing one's security is not building formal organizations for collective action—since this inevitably runs into conflict with the employer—but relying on the informal networks into which workers are born. These most commonly are networks of kin, caste, ethnicity, race, and so on. Since workers essentially inherit these connections ready-made, they become a natural source of support in normal times and especially in times of dearth. It is an irony of bourgeois society that, far from dissolving these extramarket ties, as Marx announced with such flourish in *The Communist Manifesto*, its pressures incline workers to cling to them with a desperate ferocity. It is important to note that these networks do not operate simply as material support societies. They also become a means of exerting control over the labor market and, through that, reducing the level of competition for employment. It is not just that jobs are secured through one's friends, family, or caste. It is that these connections are used to hoard job opportunities, sometimes by force, for members of one's own network. But this only intensifies a class orientation in which one's welfare is secured by forms of association unrelated to class. Indeed, organized competition in the labor market through such ties has the effect of intensifying the divisions within the class. It runs directly against the principle of class organization.

Interest Aggregation

A second obstacle to class formation is what Offe and Wiesenthal describe as the problem of interest heterogeneity.[8] It is simple enough to suggest that workers have an interest in creating associations to bargain over the terms of their exchange with capital. But workers suffer from a particular liability when considering this exchange. Unlike capital, which can be separated from the person of the employer, labor power cannot be separated from the person of the worker. When she bargains over the exchange of her laboring activity, she immediately discovers that several elements of her well-being are directly implicated in the calculation—the intensity of work, the length of the workday, the level of the wage, health benefits, pensions, and so on. Organizations created for collective action are thus saddled with the task of seeking agreement among large numbers of workers on these different dimensions of their welfare.

A second and equally daunting obstacle is that, in the case of some workers, collective organization might, in fact, make them *worse* off. This is because some workers are able to secure especially lucrative terms for themselves—perhaps due to possessing scarce skills or social connections—that make an individual bargaining strategy far more lucrative for them than a collective one. In the preceding case, collective action would call for prioritizing one set of goals from a larger list of broadly congruent ones, but in this case, it would call for some workers *subordinating* their immediate welfare to the larger agenda. Of course, in the longer run, these workers would also benefit in many ways from the security and leverage conferred by membership in the association, but the reduction in immediate welfare would be real, and they may quite rationally decline to join. Hence, if they are to be brought into the fold, they must make their decisions on a calculus substantially different than that of their colleagues.

Free Riding

A third hurdle—and perhaps the most debilitating of all—is the well-known problem of free riding. Because the terms and benefits won by these associations are made available to all their members regardless of the extent of each member's contribution, it generates a perverse incentive. Since every worker knows she will benefit if the association succeeds in its goals regardless of her individual participation in it, but she will also be no worse off if she shirks, this creates an enormous incentive for her to pass off the costs of participation to others. The result is that the effort to build associational power has to contend with workers' constant tendency to refrain from participating.

Free riding is a phenomenon common to any situation where public goods require collective action. But in a situation of generalized vulnerability and mutual competition—as is characteristic of workers' structural position—it becomes especially debilitating. It is not just that the individual worker will incur a cost if she decides to contribute to forging a class association. It is that the cost might be so high as to threaten her livelihood and thereby her economic security. The chances of having to incur this cost are, in fact, quite high since employers expend considerable effort in monitoring and then rooting out employees who show any inclination to create class organizations. Hence, even while wage laborers have a rich history of overcoming free-riding problems outside the workplace, where the risks attached to the effort are lower, it is much harder to do so at work, where the risks are so much greater—magnifying the general dilemma.

All three mechanisms are intrinsically connected to the class structure; they are a necessary component of it. All three also have the effect of *reinforcing* the atomizing effect of the labor market and *diluting* the impulse toward collective action and class consciousness. They converge to make it more attractive to workers to eschew collective strategies and opt instead for individualized defense of their basic welfare. This happens because adopting more individualized strategies incurs fewer direct costs—all the costs of time and money that go into building a union and then sustaining it—and also takes on fewer risks, such as the risk of losing employment if discovered or if they lose in their more militant tactics.

Hence, even though workers can, in certain conditions, forge the collective identity required by class struggle, they have to overcome all the structural forces that constantly pull them apart. Far from falling into a teleological account of class formation, a careful delineation of the system's basic structure leads to the opposite conclusion: that there is no easy road from Marx's class in itself to a class for itself. Indeed, the puzzle now becomes quite different from the one imputed to class analysis by its critics. Instead of having to answer why the class structure fails to impel workers toward class struggle, the challenge is to explain how working-class associational power and the pursuit of collective class strategies are achieved at all. This is the focus of the next section, and, as I argue, it is where cultural phenomena play a crucial role.

2.4

Bringing Culture Back In

Class formation occurs when workers seek out collective strategies to defend their well-being, as opposed to individualized ones that are normally more attractive. This requires, in turn, either that the mechanisms that channel their energies away from collective organization are weakened or that workers increase their willingness to incur the sacrifice entailed in organizing. These are two analytically distinct solutions to the problem of class formation, each attacking one of the two elements that jointly affect the outcome. The first dampens the effect of the external environment in which workers make their judgments; the other changes the moral calculus on which workers make their judgments about the external environment.

Workers sometimes find themselves in situations where the baseline obstacles to class organization are not as strong. Thus, workers who are more skilled, and hence harder to replace, are less vulnerable to employer retaliation if they seek to create class organizations.[9] But naturally occurring advantages like these are not common; even where they are, they are not, in themselves, sufficient. Even in cases where workers are handed some degree of insulation from the normal obstacles to class formation, it is never enough to neutralize the risks that organization entails. Hence, workers never have a garden path to self-organization, simply by virtue of their occupation or location. They might have their leverage against their employers increased, but it never rises to equality; they might find it easier to find common ground, but technical change constantly disrupts whatever accord they hammer out among themselves; and even while their contribution of time and effort might be reduced, it never goes down to zero, so the inclination to shirk remains attractive. It requires something more than serendipity for workers to generate stable and enduring class organizations.

The indispensable ingredient, in addition to a favorable external environment, is *cultural*—a shift in workers' normative orientation from individualistic to solidaristic. This flows directly from the fact that, when taking on the burdens of organizing, each worker is being urged to sacrifice scarce resources willingly for an undertaking that might very well, and often does, result in failure. Free riding is the most attractive response from an individual standpoint—hence avoiding it requires that workers include in their calculus the welfare of their peers, rather than simply their own welfare. They have to make their valuation of possible outcomes at least partly on how it will affect their peers; this stems from a sense of obligation and what they owe to the collective good. This is the essence of solidarism, of course, and it is no accident that "solidarity" has been the slogan of the labor movement across the world since its inception. In directing every worker to see the welfare of her peers as of direct concern to herself, a solidaristic ethos counteracts the individuating effects normally generated by capitalism. In so doing, it enables the creation of the collective identity that, in turn, is the cultural accompaniment to class struggle.[10]

It is important to note that creating a solidaristic ethos typically requires conscious intervention—it is not automatically generated by the class structure. Elements of mutuality and empathy are, of course, an everyday part of working-class life. In the workplace, workers often collaborate in various ways to defend themselves against managerial authority. Sometimes it is tacit and unsaid—as when they refuse to inform on one another or pick up the slack for less productive colleagues. At other times it is more explicit—as when workers cooperate to engage in a slowdown, create mutual aid societies, and so on. But these forms of cooperation are often ephemeral and dependent on particular constellations of individuals; most importantly, because they lack an organizational ballast, they do not generate bonds of trust strong and enduring enough to consistently overcome the centrifugal forces pulling workers apart. Workers know that they can rely on their colleagues for sympathy in normal circumstances—but it is never clear how far this reliance can go and how deep the trust can be.

For a culture of solidarity to become part of workers' strategic orientation requires conscious direction and agency. In its weakest form, this means a set of routines inside and outside work designed to encourage the building of relationships and, through these, the sense of trust and mutual obligation that might sustain class organizing—monthly picnics, occasional meetings to air grievances, church events, cultural productions like plays and concerts, and so forth. All these are examples of culture-generating actions initiated by organizers that stop short of creating an organization. They often happen in contexts where it is simply too dangerous to create a real workers' association—as in much of the Global South even today—or as a lead-up to a formal organization.

A stronger form of cultural intervention, of course, comes from creating a formal organization like a trade union or party, which encompasses many of the informal routines practiced in its absence but goes beyond them in the construction of a working-class identity. Organizations take up much of what is practiced in these informal routines, but they give them a permanence and structure, making them an enduring part of working-class life. Even more importantly, they link the workers' collective pursuit of their welfare to collective decision-making about strategy. Spontaneous empathy and informal routines have the effect of generating a certain amount of trust among workers but provide no reliable mechanism for coordinating their actions. Organizations provide a basis for greater trust and coordination because they are backed by a kind of institutional promise of support to their members. Just as importantly, because decisions are made in deliberative and democratic settings, they have legitimacy even with those who vote against the decisions. Hence, when the call for action goes out in the form of a strike or a slowdown, it is taken less as a command from above than as a self-exhortation.

2.5

Culture Constrained

The preceding argument highlighted the role of identity and culture in class formation. In that respect, it converges with the stream of social theory that emphasizes the ideological and discursive dimensions of the process. However, it differs in the placement of cultural construction within the overall dynamic. While the cultivation of class identity requires the creation of certain norms and values among workers, that process, in my argument, is constrained by their material interests—it is not entirely an ideological construction.

The sense of mutual identification that class formation requires is not created out of whole cloth, and it does not create an entirely new political calculus. It is built on, and continues to be constrained by, material interests. Hence, even while workers can and do operate with a sense of obligation for the welfare of their peers, this rarely displaces a regard for their own well-being. Relatedly, while workers can be enjoined to undertake risks and sacrifices for the pursuit of a collective goal, their willingness to sacrifice does not mutate into outright altruism. Both the more extreme orientations are possible, of course; they are typically the defining qualities of people known as organizers or, in a horrible bit of social-science jargon, "political entrepreneurs." These members of the class build their lives around their dedication to class organization—at enormous personal cost and at often at great risk. But the very fact that they stand out as a distinct layer within the class is evidence that they are anything but typical. The basic task of organizers is not to urge everyone else to be like them—since they know this is a lost cause. It is, rather, to persuade their peers that the organizations and campaigns they are advocating are desirable and possible. There will be some risk, and the participants will incur some costs, but they are justified because of the promised gains—in security, wages, autonomy, and so on. Solidarity does not evolve into altruism, and the willingness to sacrifice does not amount to an embrace of martyrdom.

This enduring relevance of material interests is apparent in several dimensions of working-class organization. Many pillars of trade unionism are primarily geared toward reducing the individual costs that go into collective action. This is classically evidenced in the construction of a strike fund, with the purpose of tiding workers over in the event of a work stoppage. The fund operates as a kind of insurance scheme workers pay into that comes into effect in the event of a strike. The reason every union tries to build one is eminently practical—it is a recognition of the fact that their members will not engage in a campaign simply based on principle or identity. Their willingness to commit is disciplined by their judgment of the toll it will take on them—their ability to incur the costs it will entail. Institutions like strike funds are the material supports upon which solidarity is built.

So workers base their judgments, in some measure, on what they are being asked to do. But they also assess the practicality of what they are doing it *for*—that is, the goals of the campaign. Workers assess a campaign not only on the absolute costs they are being asked to bear but also on the realizability of the goals. There are limits beyond which they judge the costs as not justified by the likelihood of success. They will perceive a certain level of sacrifice as reasonable if they deem the goal to be achievable while the same level of sacrifice will be unacceptable if the goal is feared to be unrealistic. Of course, there is no science to assessing which goals are achievable, and hence present an acceptable level of risk, and which are not. Judgments about this sometimes turn out to be mistaken; when they are, it can lead to a loss of trust in the organization and hence a decline in its legitimacy. Political organizers thus face the following challenge: If their judgments about the realism of campaigns are accurate, it can initiate a virtuous cycle in which success breeds workers' trust in the organization and in one another, which then makes it possible to undertake more ambitious campaigns, which feeds back into the strength of the class organization. But if their assessments are wrong and the pursuit of overly ambitious goals leads to defeat, it can result in a loss of trust, demoralization, a disinclination toward solidarity, and a return to a defensive, individualistic orientation by the membership.

These aspects of class organizations show again that workers can *rationally* choose *not* to undertake the arduous path of organizing. Classical Marxism often presented the situation as if the only reasonable choice was for workers to forge class associations. When it was found that the inclination to embrace this strategy was at best uneven within the class, some early Marxists attributed this to a collapse of rationality among workers—this was the theory of false consciousness. In other words, they insisted that Marxist theory was right but the *workers* were mistaken in their judgment about their own interests. It is, of course, true that anyone can be misled or mistaken in their understanding of whether or not they are being harmed. But a theory that relies on attributing a systematic failure in judgment to large groups is indulging in a rather spectacular bit of special pleading.

A more plausible conceptualization of the problem is this—when workers contemplate the attractiveness of class association, they are implicitly comparing its feasibility against the option of an individualized resistance strategy, and each of these options has something to recommend it. While the associational option holds a promise of more leverage against their employer and hence the possibility of material gains, it also exposes the workers to new risks and a series of costs they would not otherwise have to bear, ceteris paribus. Organizers, in a sense, ask workers to choose between two strategies, each of which comes with its own risk / reward matrix. The individualized route carries lower immediate risks but also exposes the worker to continued managerial despotism and lower economic welfare, whereas the collective strategy promises more power and better economic outcomes but at a greater cost and risk. The hard work of organizing is not simply to exhort workers into action; it is to attract them into membership by changing the risk / reward matrix that normally *disinclines* them from joining or participating in campaigns, thereby making the collective strategy a more attractive option. If the costs are too great or the campaigns continue to run aground, solidarity will either never arise or will begin to erode. Workers then begin to drift toward the safety of keeping their heads down and returning to the safer, more individualized strategy of reproduction.

Hence, class formation requires an ongoing process of cultural intervention, but its effectiveness is conditional on aligning it with workers' material interests. This account of culture in class politics acknowledges that class identities are not a natural or necessary outgrowth of the class structure. Indeed, the implications of my argument turn the classic Marxist account on its head. In the classical account, the class structure is taken to generate class consciousness, which, in turn, induces workers to build class organizations. I have argued that, in fact, class consciousness is the *consequence of class* organization. Since the latter is an arduous process, highly vulnerable to disruption and precarious at its foundation, so is the formation of class identity. Hence, the fact that workers often do not build their identities around their class location is not evidence for the weakness of a materialist class theory—it is what the theory should predict.

2.6
Back to Structure

For some time now, the putative teleology of structural class theory has been viewed as its biggest weakness. In this chapter, I have tried to show that it is possible to accept much of the edifice of the classical theory while eschewing its teleological conclusions. One can accept that laboring groups experience harms as a consequence of their class location; one can also accept that these harms motivate them to resist, as Marx insisted. But both these points can be taken on board without the additional argument that the resistance would necessarily take an organized and collective form. In fact, the more rational course of action is for workers to tend toward an individual resistance because of the cost / risk matrix they encounter in organizing collectively. If this is so, we have a materialist explanation for the very phenomenon culturalists have taken to be devastating to the theory.

The implication of my argument is that classical Marxists erred, not in their fidelity to a structural class theory but in their failure to fully theorize its implications. What that theory predicts, I suggest, is the very contingency in class formation that cultural theory has insisted upon. But while my argument does align with the culturalists' embrace of contingency in class formation, it does not amount to an endorsement of the *radical* contingency some of them espouse. Politics still runs along grooves firmly set by the class structure. First, the uncertainty of building working-class associations does not make power itself a contingent affair. It merely reduces the weight on *one* side of the equation, the side of labor. The power of employers remains very much in place; indeed, it is amplified by the enfeeblement of labor's organizational strength. Hence, it is not power itself that is a contingent affair, for it is rests securely with the capitalist class; all that is uncertain is labor's ability to build its counter to it.

Furthermore, even on labor's side, the important contribution of cultural work does not mean class identities and organization are purely a cultural affair. They remained constrained by the workers' material interests, which are, in turn, set by their structural location. As I argued in Section 2.5, no amount of exhortation or ideological indoctrination will induce workers, in large numbers, to ventures that are unlikely to succeed in improving their situation. In cases where organizations fail to abide by this dictum, they will find that they gradually lose their support, start hemorrhaging members, and spiral into a decline. Identification with a political strategy or the class organization thus operates within material constraints.

Two facts are especially important for what is to come. First, the challenges to collective action are not distributed equally across classes. Employers not only face lower costs but are absolved of the very need to organize collectively in many situations. On the other side, workers face both a greater need to organize and much higher costs in pursuing it. This injects a fundamental imbalance into the power struggle between them. Second, the asymmetry is built into the class structure itself. It is not an artifact of a particular variety of capitalism or an epoch within it. It is the baseline reality of the system against which all the institutional innovations within the labor movement have evolved over the past century: the class structure itself places impediments to working-class formation.

If the contingency of class formation can be traced back to the class structure itself, it has some very important implications for the explanation of capitalist stability. Recall that, for the Marxist framework, as well as for its critics, the road to instability leads through class formation. For most class-based accounts of modern politics, the traversal out of capitalism—into socialism or some other order—is effectuated through class formation. For the postwar theorists of the New Left, if the obstacle to class formation was cultural in essence, it was also the mechanism that explained the durability of the system. If capitalism survived, it was because certain facts about working-class culture, or the dominant culture, prevented the working class from organizing itself, thereby securing the rule of capital. These cultural facts were therefore central to the explanation for how the dominant class maintained its power and, through that, also sustained the system's reproduction. But if the basic obstacles to class formation are not cultural, and are instead structural or economic, this will also affect the explanation of how the system endures or how the dominant class secures its rule. We now have the possibility of an alternative and more materialist theory of capitalist stability, building on the newer theory of class formation. This is what I explore in the next chapter.

3

Consent, Coercion, and Resignation

The arguments of the first two chapters have positioned us to revisit one of the central issues for contemporary social theory—how does capitalism survive? Classical Marxism confidently asserted that capitalism's own logic would lead inexorably to the organization of the working class and the overthrow of the system. Why, then, had it not? For postwar critical theorists, especially the early protagonists of the cultural turn, materialist class theory lacked the resources to answer this question. This theory, derived from Marx and Lenin, had assumed that the clash of material interests would be sufficient to unleash an escalating spiral of political conflict. It rested on the assumption that the forms of consciousness—of self-identification—would emerge within labor sooner or later, even if the path was a torturous one. Critical theorists charged that classical Marxists had never seriously considered the possibility of workers having multiple forms of consciousness—social identities that extended beyond those of class—and hence forging allegiances that sustained the system rather than threatened it. This, in turn, was taken to be a consequence of classical Marxism's general demotion of culture and ideology. Culture, after all, was "in the superstructure" and hence unable to overcome the contradictions located in the economic structure. It followed that the incorporation of the working class into postwar capitalism was anomalous from the standpoint of classical Marxism.

The theorists trying to understand the phenomenon appeared to see only two choices—either abandon structural class theory or refashion it so that ideology and culture were imported into its foundation. Many intellectuals did, in fact, take the decline of economic conflict as a decisive refutation of classical Marxism and turned away from class analysis altogether. But for some of the most influential currents of social theory, a more appealing alternative was to retain the basic anchor in class, albeit with an elevation of culture from its subordinate role to one of central importance. Instead of treating ideology as a black box, they launched a program to explicate the mechanisms by which people were socialized into accepting their roles in the system—through media, schools, religious institutions, and so on. Several streams of theorizing converged on a broadly similar conclusion—that the key to understanding capitalism's durability was the successful generation of *consent* within the working class. And the source of this consent was ideology and culture.

In this chapter, I provide a different answer to the question of capitalism's durability. Building on the arguments in the first two chapters, I suggest that the key is not ideology but certain facts about the class structure itself. The motivation for my rejection of the cultural arguments is that, far from correcting the lacunae in the structural class theory, they are actually incompatible with it. For ideology to perform the role allotted to it, culturalists either have to assume severe and ongoing cognitive breakdown among social actors or have to whisk away the basic facts about class, which they claim to accept as valid. It is not surprising, then, that so many of the proponents of the cultural turn ended up letting go of their anchoring in class— for the argument from ideological consent can only sit uneasily with the latter.

My argument proceeds in two steps. First, I suggest that insofar as active consent is important in the stabilization of capitalism, it is not based on culture or socialization but on the coordination of material interests. Workers are persuaded to accept the system as legitimate, not by dint of ideology but because of how it aligns with their well-being. This part of the argument accepts a role for consent but offers a materialist counter to the prevailing accounts. But second, I offer that while consent contributes to the system's durability, it is not its basic source. The more fundamental mechanism for capitalism's stability is workers' *resignation* to their situation. And they resign themselves to it because of the constraints on class formation as explained in Chapter 2. The myriad obstacles to collective action incline workers to resist as individuals, and not through mutual coordination, which sometimes improves the situation of particular workers but does little to alter the structural inequality in capacity between the two classes. This, in turn, maintains the dominance of the employer class, and workers see little choice but to adjust their expectations and their strategies to their subordinate position. Which is to say that they have little choice but to resign themselves to the basic facts about their situation. Hence, they accept their class position, even though they may not deem it desirable or legitimate. I conclude with an account of how ideology still plays an important role in this proves—but as an effect of capitalist stability, not its cause.

3.1

The Turn to Consent

At a landmark 1983 conference in Illinois, Stuart Hall delivered a series of eight lectures on the evolution and contribution of cultural
studies in postwar England. Hall was one of the pivotal figures in the
British New Left, director of the legendary Center for Contemporary
Cultural Studies in Birmingham, and one of the most influential cultural theorists of his time.[1] In his opening presentation, he described
the motivation behind the turn to culture by British intellectuals in
the 1950s:

> It is important to understand that the concept of culture was pro-
> posed, not as the answer to some grand theoretical question, but as a
> response to a very *concrete* political problem and question: what hap-
> pened to the working class under conditions of economic affluence?[2]

The actual question was even more specific than Hall's construal
of it: why was the intensely combative labor movement of the interwar
years so easily absorbed into the system? In the prior passage, Hall
seems to have the rudiments of an answer—it is connected to the material prosperity of postwar capitalism and, hence, to economic conditions. But he and his peers found this explanation inadequate. While
economic changes were certainly relevant, he recalls, "it was also per-
fectly clear that the major transformations were not so much political
and economic as cultural and social."[3] The challenge, then, was to generate an account of how the "cultural and social" facts about modern
society conspired to fasten the working class to the system and thereby
mute, or even overturn, the antagonism between the classes.

As Hall recounts, the people taking up this question were not
scions of the British intellectual establishment. They were the emergent

figures of the New Left, ascending to intellectual maturity and eager to resolve the puzzle as a prelude to more effective political engagement.[4] To this generation, the natural framework for analyzing the political conjuncture was classical Marxism. But they soon concluded that the framework was ill-suited to the task. The problem was that the Marxist framework was wedded to the base-superstructure model, which gave very little efficacy to cultural phenomena. Culture, for Marxists, was "fully and intimately determined" by economic relations and hence "gave very little room to the efficacy of the superstructures themselves."[5] Hall comes back to this repeatedly in his lecture—the New Left's conviction that it would have to launch "an assault on the problem of the inadequacy of the base-superstructure model understood as a strong theory of determination" to make sense of the postwar stabilization of capitalism.[6]

It was not just the British New Left that came to this conclusion. Several of the most influential streams of social theory converged on the view that the key to capitalism's reproduction resided in ideology and culture. Two of the most influential texts of the Frankfurt school, Max Horkheimer and Theodor Adorno's *The Dialectic of Enlightenment* and, later, Herbert Marcuse's *One-Dimensional Man*, focused on the means by which the working class was culturally absorbed into capitalism, thereby blunting the system's latent contradictions. The mechanisms were different—for the former, it was through the working of the "culture industry," while for Marcuse it was from the psychic benefits of consumption. But, in both, the impulse was to locate the explanation in "the superstructure," as Hall would have described it, not in the economic structure itself.

Postwar intellectuals found their anchor in the work of Antonio Gramsci more than any other theorist. If explaining capitalism's stabilization required an analytical shift from the economy to culture, then

Gramsci's work promised to reap dividends, for, as Noberto Bobbio explained, he was the theorist of the "superstructure" par excellence.[7] At the core of the Gramscian turn were two propositions: one that was generic to the intellectual scene, and thereby enabled the New Left to recognize the Sardinian as a kindred spirit, and the other more specific to his work, thereby imbuing it with an apparent originality.

Gramsci's first proposition was that, even if Marx was right in supposing that the dominant class drew its income from the labor of subordinate groups, this was not sufficient to maintain the former's political supremacy. To maintain its grip over power, it could not simply rely on coercion or violence. These may suffice for brief periods as expedients, but in the longer run, dominant classes would have to elicit the consent of other classes to their rule. The idea that political power, even in class society, hinged on the acquisition of subordinate groups' consent was taken to be a significant innovation in the classical framework. As Hall recounted, the emergent New Left was frustrated with the Marxism it inherited but not yet ready to reject it outright. It wanted to retain its moorings in class analysis, and even in the materialism upon which the latter rested, but with a sharper focus on the role of culture. It was quite apparent to this emerging cohort of theorists that, contrary to the predictions of their mentors, the working class had become a willing participant in the postwar social order—it was not being ruled by coercion but by its own consent. And here was Gramsci, a contemporary of Lenin and Luxemburg, asserting the very proposition Hall and his peers were trying to articulate.

Gramsci's prioritization of consent drew the New Left, and later the wider intellectual community, to his work. But what propelled him to the center of the cultural turn was his description of how consent was secured. In the most common reading of his work, the means by which dominant classes elicited subordinate groups' consent was through *culture.* Gramsci drew upon a particular locution of Lenin's in the wake of the Russian Revolution of 1905. In his interventions in debates on strategy, Lenin had argued that in a country like Russia, where the industrial proletariat was only a tiny minority among the laboring classes, it could only achieve power through an alliance with the peasantry. But since the peasantry was a distinct social group whose interests were not identical to those of the working class, the alliance could only be cemented through a program that brought the classes together in the pursuit of common goals. Such a program would attract the peasantry to the working class; in so doing, it would secure the working class's *ideological hegemony* over the latter.[8]

In this model, a class secured its hegemony over kindred classes by eliciting their consent to its program and outlook. It was intended to describe a *horizontal* relation between classes—either among exploiting classes or among the exploited. Gramsci's innovation was to expand it to describe the *vertical* relation between exploiters and exploited. The version that was most widely accepted, and thereby became the conventional understanding of Gramsci's contribution, is very effectively summarized by Martin Carnoy:

> For [Gramsci] neither force *nor the logic of capitalist production* could explain the consent that production enjoyed among the subordinate classes. Rather, *the explanation for this consent lay in the power of consciousness and ideology.* . . . Hegemony involves the successful attempt by the dominant class to use its political, moral, and intellectual leadership to establish its view of the world as all-inclusive and universal and to shape the interests and needs of the subordinate class.[9]

Thus, hegemony referred to a state of affairs in which dominant classes were able to secure their rule by eliciting the ideological consent of the masses. It wasn't just that ideology was the means by which the latter articulated their subordination to the system but, rather, that it was the mechanism by which the subordination was achieved in the first place. By dint of its intellectual and moral leadership, the dominant class was able to go beyond merely expressing or coordinating the interests of the subordinate classes and could actually "shape [their] interests and needs." This reading of Gramsci had him reversing the causal relation between interests and ideology, as understood by classical Marxists. Whereas, for materialists, ideology was more a medium through which interests were articulated, this reading of Gramsci inverted that relationship so that the former actually constructed the latter. In so doing, it placed culture at the very core of a theory of social stability.

The passage from Carnoy is significant because he does not present it as his reading of the original text. He is summarizing what he takes to be a widely held reading of the Sardinian Marxist—a sort of consensus view, relatively uncontroversial. As I observe in the following, there were other interpretations of what the concept of hegemony entailed for Gramsci. But there is little doubt that Carnoy's presentation encapsulated the most commonly held understanding of the theory—hegemony was based on consent, and consent was secured through culture. This proposition led to a fecund research program, across the moral sciences, focused on how media, educational institutions, religion, and so forth all function to create, disseminate, and reproduce the ideologies by which actors are absorbed into the system. In a very real way, by the 1980s, the early New Left's conviction regarding the role of culture in capitalism's stabilization had become a kind of common sense. The question remains, however—is the theory persuasive?

3.2

Consent and the Reality of Class

There is little doubt that the acquisition of working-class consent is important to the stabilization of capitalism. In drawing attention to this and placing it at the core of their scholarly agenda, the New Left and the broader intelligentsia influenced by it made an important contribution to political theory. The issue, however, is not whether consent plays a role in stabilizing the system but whether it is the fundamental source of the latter. In what follows, I suggest that it is not and that its role is subsidiary to another, more mundane mechanism; furthermore, I argue that even while working-class consent may be important to the dominant class's power, they do not acquire it by dint of ideological persuasion, moral and intellectual leadership, and so forth but by their ability to align the interests of the subordinate classes with their own. In short, I develop an account of capitalist stability that reconstructs hegemony on materialist lines and demotes the place of consent—even in its reconstructed materialist form—to a secondary role. Finally, I suggest that insofar as ideology does play a role, it is more as a reaction to the system's stabilization and not as its source. Ideology is the medium by which actors *respond* to their location in the structure—not the factor that binds them to it.

To fix our thoughts, it is important to first be clear about what the concept of consent is intended to convey. In all its uses, it signals that an actor has given his assent to a particular state of affairs. To consent to something is to signal that you willingly accept it. But this acceptance can of be of two kinds:

- *Active consent:* One that deems the situation intrinsically desirable and therefore legitimate.
- *Passive consent:* One that deems the situation regrettable but unavoidable.

The first is an eager acceptance, the latter a grudging one. Hence, when I agree to a substantial improvement in my monetary compensation at work, I am offering an *active* consent. It is a state of affairs I deem intrinsically desirable and therefore legitimate. But if I am asked to take a pay cut because my employer is experiencing a drop in his revenue, I am likely to offer only my *passive* consent because, all else being equal, it is a state of affairs I would rather avoid. I accept it under duress—because the alternative is even more odious.

In the literature on class domination, when the concept is deployed to describe the orientation of subordinate groups, it is meant to convey an active consent. The idea is that, by dint of ideological or cultural incorporation, the working class comes to regard the social order as legitimate and, in some way, desirable. It consents to its rule not because it feels it has no choice but because its subjectivity is shaped by the dominant class's ideological influence. This is what Carnoy means when he suggests it is "neither force nor the logic of capitalist production" that is behind working class consent but "the power of . . . ideology." In our locution, Carnoy is drawing a contrast between active and passive consent and saying quite emphatically that it is the former that sustains dominant-class hegemony over laboring groups.[10]

Now, the argument from active consent faces some daunting challenges. The most fundamental is that it is not easy to reconcile with the description of the class structure that most every theorist of hegemony implicitly or explicitly endorses. Recall that capitalist stability is puzzling because of the facts about its underlying structure. For the New Left, the Gramscians, the Frankfurt School, and most other critical theorists, the puzzle is motivated by their antecedent description of the system's structural dynamics—the fact that it is based on class domination and exploitation. The question is posed in terms

of how a class maintains its domination over another—how it repro-
duces its rule over another. The entire enterprise of the cultural turn
was launched to answer why class conflict was not occurring. But the
reason that the absence of conflict is anomalous is that the system is
taken to rest on processes that *ought* to incite the working class into
action. Hence, to even pose the question is to signal that you have accepted the classical Marxist account of the capitalist class structure.

Let us briefly review what that account entails. In the description
of capitalism accepted by all theorists of hegemony, the class structure inflicts certain harms on the subordinate class. These were the
dimensions of the employment relation explored in Chapter 2. First,
there is the experience at work. The employer maximizes his profits
by extracting the maximal units of labor as is feasible in the time allotted. This is experienced by workers as a steady demand to speed
up and intensify the pace of work, a demand often imposed without
regard for the effect it has on employee well-being. As long as replacement workers are available, the employer is free to impose a work
regimen that prioritizes his profit maximization over the welfare of
his employee. This is experienced by workers as a *harm*—a direct
assault on their well-being. Second, there is the more generic loss of
autonomy, of which subordination to the onerous pace of work is just
one dimension. As Elizabeth Anderson has persuasively argued, the
workplace in capitalism is something akin to a private government—
a kind of despotism in situ—wherein employers exercise a wide range
of arbitrary powers over their employees.[11] For the duration of the
workday, the employee is subject to the authority of his employer
over a gamut of basic functions—where to stand, when to sit, who
to talk to, when to eat, when to go to the bathroom, and so on. This
has, across time and space, been a source of tremendous resentment
in the working class—showing up not only as a demand for specific

freedoms on the workplace but, time and again, as a generic demand for "respect" or "dignity."[12]

Apart from the injuries and indignities of work are the terms on which the labor contract is secured. Prime among these is the baseline sense of insecurity imposed by wage labor. It is an irony of capitalism that while workers seek out employment as a remedy to their material insecurity, the wage relation does not so much erase that insecurity as it does institutionalize it. To work for a wage is to face the constant threat of dismissal. From the employer's standpoint, this is the basis on which he can make demands on his employee at all; without it, his property rights over material assets are of little use since he loses the authority to direct his labor as market conditions demand. But from the employee's standpoint, the threat of dismissal endows his employer with an arbitrary power over him—the loss of autonomy just acknowledged prior—but it also destabilizes much of his life outside the workplace in that the rest of his life choices have to be subordinated to ensuring that he prioritizes his attractiveness to a current or future employer. The loss of power at work is complemented by a general anxiety at home.

Finally, there is the issue of the wage level itself—another aspect of the terms on which the employment relation is secured. Since there is no mechanism to ensure that productivity increases will translate into higher wages, the worker perceives the call for more effort not as an exhortation but as a threat. It comes with a warning that if he does not deliver, he could lose his position to a rival in the labor market or any forthcoming pay increases will not redound to him. Even more, if it turns out that his bargaining power is slight, he is easily replaceable, or the general level of organization of the class is weak, she will be vulnerable to long periods of either stagnant or falling living standards. The general character of employment becomes one in which the demands for more sacrifice remain constant, while the rewards in terms of material improvement become highly contingent.

These elements of the employment relation are built into the class structure. They vary in pitch and intensity, but they cannot be over-turned as long as production is organized along capitalist lines. It follows that these are also facts that must be accepted by the votaries of ideological consent, insofar as the very question they are posing is set against the backdrop of this description of the class structure.

But if they are, in fact, taken on board, the argument from consent has to explain how the simple fact of ideology can inure workers to the harms generated by class domination. It is, of course, true that schools, religious institutions, the media, and the state present the status quo as legitimate; that the poor are socialized into this view of the world; and that dominant classes try to capitalize on their "moral and intellectual leadership." But this is all a description of indoctrination *effort*. It does not and cannot predict the degree to which the latter is *successful*. That outcome—the degree to which the ideology is internalized—is dependent on factors independent of the indoctrination effort. It will hinge upon the workers' own dispositions, their critical faculties, and the presence of other, countervailing ideological practices—above all, it will depend on the workers' actual experience of their class situation and if that experience confirms or undermines the ideology's framing of the system as legitimate and desirable.

As thinking, reasoning actors, workers cannot be assumed to pas-sively internalize the worldview expressed by dominant institutions. True, actors are in some fashion "interpellated" by the dominant ideology, as Louis Althusser describes it.[13] Their subjectivity is at least partially acquired through the codes disseminated by dominant institutions, and this encourages them to view the world in a certain way. But no theory of ideological reproduction can stop at that point, as Althusser's rather functionalist take does. There is also the matter of people's actual experience of their status as workers, which can either reinforce or undermine the claims to legitimacy propagated by the ideology. The challenge for culturalists is to explain how it might be that workers who experience the harms and indignities attached to the employment relation, as described prior, are willing to actively embrace them by dint of *ideology alone*—to see it as legitimate simply because they have been told it is. Culturalists are in the embarrassing position of claiming implicitly that while *they* can discern the exploitative—and hence unjust—character of the employment relation, the actors who are, *in fact*, being exploited, who are experiencing its brute facts, are not capable of doing so.

None of this is to deny the salience of popular consent as an element contributing to social stability. There is little doubt that workers' active consent contributes to some degree to the construction of hegemony. What is in doubt is that the consent can be explained on the basis of their socialization—that they embrace their place within the class structure *because* the dominant ideology tells them to. A more persuasive account would have to respect their basic capacities as conscious agents, as people aware of their situation and its consequences upon their well-being. It stands to reason that if certain practices are recognized by the theorist as being oppressive toward some social group, he should allow that members of that group might be capable of the same judgment.

3.3

The Material Basis of Consent

How might we understand workers' consent to their place in the structure if we allow that they are aware of the harms it inflicts upon them? In a series of important interventions, Adam Przeworski offered a theory based on a reading of Gramsci profoundly different from that of the culturalists.[14] He agreed with the premise that capitalism's stabilization rests substantially on the dominant class's ability to elicit the active consent of subordinate groups. But he rejected the idea that this could be based on ideology alone—or even primarily. And he emphatically rejected the notion that Gramsci held to such an account. As he explained, the culturalist readings "render Gramsci's thought intellectually trivial and politically misdirected" since they treat workers as dupes. But equally, these readings "are not sustained by the texts."[15] Przeworski argued that, for the Italian theorist, consent was articulated through an ideology but never based upon it. Its foundation was always and everywhere *economic*.[16]

On the basis of his alternative reading, Przeworski offers a more materialist account of consent. Workers only agree to their exploitation when, and if, they are able to experience real gains from it. The essence of the matter lies in the uncertainties of the wage relation. Workers, as observed in Section 2.1, seek out waged employment to reduce the material insecurity created by their class position. But the irony is that, once they find employment, it does not so much eliminate their insecurity as institutionalize it. Because of his control over the means of production, all matters regarding income, the pace of work, the duration of employment, and so on are in the hands of the employer and subject to his priorities. Thus, the various dimensions of workers' well-being remain substantially out of their control and subject to an arbitrary authority, leaving their future fundamentally uncertain.

Przeworski suggests that capitalists are able to acquire active consent from the labor force when they agree to reduce the myriad insecurities of the employment relation. They submit to a binding arrangement: in exchange for a certain level of work effort and cooperation, they commit a certain proportion of their profits to steady increases in workers' remuneration. In Przeworski's argument, the emphasis is on wages—workers offer their consent when they are assured that their work effort will translate into rising wage levels over time.[17] But it can be elevated to a more general proposition—namely, that workers offer their consent when they are able to bind capitalists to using a portion of current profits to generate future gains for them—in some combination of income, work conditions, job security, and so forth. Thus, workers agree to cooperate on the condition that the terms of the exchange be expanded so that the arbitrary nature of the employer's power over them is reduced.

This theory of consent displaces ideology with the coordination of material interests as the central mechanism. Przeworski was by no means the only scholar to reject the culturalist interpretation of Gramsci.[18] And as I argue in the following, he was correct to do so. But his interventions are significant in that he did not stop at the textual analysis. He offered a theory consistent with the "materialist Gramsci" but far more elaborate in its details. Its advantage is that it does not require workers to suffer from a sustained cognitive break-down. They offer their active consent because, under conditions of the political exchange with capitalists, they are able to effectuate an ongoing increase in their economic welfare. Far from simply being passive objects of exploitation, they are at least partially able to make the system work for them. It makes the employment relation inch closer to being a positive-sum game, hence providing the dominant class's hegemony with a material, and sustainable, basis.

The problem with Przeworski's argument is that, even if it is accepted, it cannot provide a theory of consent across time and space in capitalism. This is because it requires a considerable degree of organized, coordinated action by the working class. It presumes the existence of intermediate organizations such as trade unions, which serve to both organize the class and negotiate the terms of their employment with capitalists. While this certainly explains hegemonic stability in some countries and in some periods of capitalist history, it leaves much of the global experience of capitalism out of its scope. For much of its early history in western Europe, the working class was not organized into unions, and in the Global South, it never has been. Today, even in advanced countries, the extent of class organization is once again very uneven, making the institutional preconditions for Przeworski's model tenuous at best. Hence, while it is certainly true that a coordinated political exchange between labor and capital can generate a consensual order, it is at best a special and limited case of hegemony. The more general case has to be one in which workers consent *without* the help of intermediate organizations.

In fact, a theory of this kind is what Gramsci offers in his *Notebooks.* Whereas Przeworski presumes an organized working class in his account, Gramsci does not, which makes the two theories somewhat different in their description of the material basis of consent. In Przeworski's story, consent becomes available when workers *impose* a political exchange upon the capitalists via their class organizations; however, as I show in the following, for Gramsci, capitalists elicit consent when they *attract* subordinate classes to their side, even if the latter are disorganized, by virtue of their stewardship of societal productive forces. Gramsci offers a very clear exposition of this basic theory in the essay "The Intellectuals," but it is confirmed time and again throughout the manuscripts.

Gramsci's account suggests that the dominant class is able to secure a "political, moral and intellectual leadership" of the subordinate classes, as Carnoy describes it. But this leadership is not based on ideology or discourse. Gramsci argues emphatically that "though hegemony is ethical-political, it must also be economic, must *necessarily* be based on the decisive function exercised by the leading group in the *decisive nucleus of economic activity.*"[19] In this process of securing the consent of the masses, Gramsci describes the function of intellectuals as "organizational and connective"—they are intermediaries between the emergent dominant class and the masses. They don't "shape the interests and needs" of the subordinate groups, as Carnoy would have it, but *coordinate* those interests with those of the dominant class. Hence, hegemony is based on

> the "spontaneous" consent given by the great masses of the population *to the general direction imposed on social life* by the dominant fundamental group; this consent is "historically" caused by the prestige (and consequent confidence) which the dominant group enjoys *because of its position and function in the world of production.*[20]

Note that there is a powerful impulse toward consent, not because of an institutionalized bargain but because of the prestige enjoyed by the dominant class; this prestige is not a cultural construction but an outgrowth of its control over the economic lifeblood of society.

The dominant class's control over the productive forces enables it to capture the political high ground. Because it is able to engineer a high rate of economic growth, it also delivers steady improvements in the economic welfare of its allies. More to the point, it is able to offer material gains without having to sacrifice its own economic interests because its economic dynamism turns what could be a zero-sum game between itself and the laboring classes into a positive-sum game. The steadily expanding economic pie supports steady economic improvements for laboring classes while also ensuring an ever-expanding surplus for their exploiters. The real prospect of these gains—the actual experience of their spread—generates the "spontaneous 'consent' given by the great masses" to the new order. This is the mechanism by which the dominant class secures its hegemony because now, on its promise to deliver real gains,

> [the] dominant group is coordinating concretely with the general interests of subordinate groups and the life of the State is seen as a continuous process of formation and superseding of unstable equilibria . . . between the interests of the fundamental group and the subordinate groups—equilibria in which the interests of the dominant group prevail but only up to a certain point, i.e. stopping short of narrowly corporate economic interest.[21]

The key to eliciting the consent of the masses is for the ruling class to coordinate its interests with those of the laboring classes, which it is able to do because its economic dynamism creates an ever-expanding economy in which real gains can be experienced across the class divide. Because it is the actor delivering the goods to the other classes, it is able to assure that its own interests "become the interests of other subordinate groups too."[22]

Both versions of the argument—Gramsci's and Przeworski's—locate the ruling class's hegemony in its economic function. The difference is that for the latter, hegemony is derived from a political exchange between labor and capital, which assumes some degree of organization within the working class. Gramsci makes no such assumption, which makes his theory a more general one. And this is intentional. He quite explicitly seeks to anchor his account in what he understands as Marx's historical sociology, the clearest expression of which is—for him, as for all the leading Marxists of his generation—the 1859 preface to the *Contribution to a Critique of Political Economy*. It is striking that, in several instances where he examines the role of politics or culture in social reproduction, Gramsci first reminds himself, and the reader, that any viable theory of it has to be consistent with the framework laid out in the preface. This is not surprising, since he describes it as "the most important authentic source for a reconstruction of the philosophy of praxis [i.e., Marxism]."[23]

In the preface, of course, Marx is at his most fiercely deterministic. He sets out his theory of history, in which the rise and decline of social orders are explained by their functionality for economic development. Gramsci's persistent and studied invocation of this document will be something of a shock to anyone schooled in the culturalist interpretation of his work. But for our purposes, two aspects are especially important. The first is that it is pitched at a very high level of generality, abstracting away from institutional variations within an economic system and instead focusing on its basic structure to uncover its fundamental properties. Marx is not interested in explaining variations within capitalism, or any system that preceded it, but rather the principles that govern the system across its various forms. Insofar as Gramsci anchors his theory of hegemony in this framework, he also seeks to ignore the institutional specificities of the system. Hence, he locates the sources of hegemony not in the contingent fact of labor's organized negotiations with capital but in the basic features of the system, with or without that organization.

Second, this is why the feature that creates the possibility of hegemony is the system's economic dynamism. In Marx's preface, social orders remain stable only so long as they successfully incubate the development of the productive forces. As their growth-enhancing capacity begins to wane, as the productive forces begin to stagnate, the system's stability also begins to weaken. Gramsci invokes one particular aspect of the preface precisely when he addresses the problem of hegemony. In explicating "the relations between structure and superstructure," he reminds us,

> Two principles must orient the discussion: 1. that no society sets itself tasks for whose accomplishment the necessary and sufficient conditions do not either already exist or are not at least beginning to emerge and develop; 2. that no society breaks down and can be replaced until it has first developed all the forms of life which are implicit in its internal relations.[24]

In another elaboration of the same idea, Gramsci describes it thus: "That no social formation disappears as long as the productive forces which have developed within it still find room for further forward movement."[25] These passages suggest that as long as the dominant class in a social order can oversee its economic development, it can also maintain its dominance, for its rule also improves the material condition of those over whom it has power. The hegemony comes from the system's capacity to widely distribute the fruits of economic growth and not from an organized agreement between labor and capital—which is the crux of Przeworski's theory. Class agency is important in this since the organic intellectuals of the dominant class create the institutional channels by which the economic gains are transferred to subordinate groups. And Gramsci allows that they can fail in it. Indeed, in the pages of the *Notebooks* that follow the explication of the two principles, he goes on to describe the various means by which dominant classes might fail in this endeavor. The point is that, for Gramsci, the class's success or failure in this regard is not just determined by the contingencies of political contestation but by the overarching "laws of development" as laid out by Marx in his preface.[26] Classes can take advantage of the space opened up by the economic circumstances, but once it begins to close, so does the room for their agency.

Hence, Gramsci's theory is system wide in scope while Przeworski's is institutionally specific. An organized political exchange might deepen a dominant class's hegemony, but it is not the basic source of the latter. What both theories have in common is that the subordinate class's consent is not based upon ideological indoctrination or culture but upon the promise of steadily improving material welfare. And because of this, neither theory has to rely on a breakdown in actors' cognitive ability or a denial of the conflict latent in the class structure. We can understand how workers might reasonably consent to their place in a capitalist system.

3.4

The Problem with Consent

Gramsci's theory is the most convincing account we have of the material basis of consent. But this does not mean it can suffice as an explanation for *capitalist stability.* Two problems, in particular, loom large: First, is economic growth really enough to overcome the perception of harm among workers? Second, is consent, even if acquired, really the central mechanism for maintaining the status quo? In what follows, I argue that the answer to both questions is negative. And if that is so— if consent cannot, in fact, be the bedrock on which capitalists secure their dominance—we need a different explanation for its durability.

Is Growth Enough to Generate Consent?

Recall that the impact of the wage contract on employees' well-being is multidimensional. There is the basic fact of income, of course, and there is no doubt that increases in productivity often translate into rising wages.[27] But that is only one aspect of the workers' class situation. Their well-being is also influenced by other facts—work intensity, safety conditions, the security of the contract, and so forth, as discussed prior.[28] Now, it stands to reason that even if gains are made along one dimension, the other dimensions may remain untouched. Hence, the perception of harms can remain among workers even if growth is translating into wage increases. The experience of work can and does remain onerous, even if the productive forces are advancing as Gramsci's theory requires, and hence the employment relation will remain conflictual even as standards of living increase. But more importantly, it is not just that improvements in one dimension might leave conditions in the other relevant ones untouched; it is that they often come at the cost of intensifying the harms experienced in the other dimensions. What is gained in one aspect of the work relation is balanced by a deterioration of conditions in the other ones.

By way of illustration, consider the length of the working day. By the late nineteenth century, labor in several European countries had won its battle for a mandated limit to the workweek. This was an unambiguous gain in a critical dimension of their well-being in that the workday was finally subjected to some regulation, bringing it down from as much as fifteen hours a day to ten and ultimately to the forty-hour week. And it had the added benefit of triggering a wave of technological innovations as employers had to seek new ways of increasing productivity now that sweating labor was off the table. This laid the basis for a more rapid increase in the real wage. But employers responded to the limit on how long they could work their employees by intensifying the pace at which they worked. By the 1930s, a number of studies found that employees were working less, but they were now also working harder. The added machines, the new organization of work, and the creation of new skills—all of which were indicators of a massive leap in the productive powers of society—were accompanied by a deterioration in the experience of work.[29]

In the same period, because of the same processes, workers also recoiled against the encroachments on their autonomy. As employers had to comply with the new limits on the workday and brought in new machinery to avoid reductions in throughput, they had to reorganize the division of labor within the factory. But this entailed a wholesale attack on their workers' autonomy. In leading industrial districts in Britain and the United States, the labor process in manufacturing was still largely under the immediate control of skilled workers. Introducing new machinery, setting new work standards, and implementing a new division of labor—all this required breaking through the barriers imposed by skilled workers' independence on the shop floor. Much of the impetus for labor organizing in the late nineteenth century came from skilled workers and was motivated by an attempt to defend their rapidly eroding autonomy. Again, a potential gain in one dimension—wages—was offset by a loss in another.[30]

It is noteworthy that the last great upheaval in labor relations came at the end of the 1960s, when wages and incomes were rising at the fastest pace in decades. In the years 1968–1973, western Europe and the United States were wracked by a series of massive strikes, the most disruptive since the end of World War II. But whereas the strikes after the war had been triggered by a backlog of demands built up under wartime conditions, the upheavals twenty-five years later were specific to that conjuncture. In the United States, they were, in fact, directly related to the increases in productivity. For even though wages were rising, the greater output on which they drew was achieved by a dramatic intensification of work.[31] The workers' disruptive job actions were a dramatic illustration of the principle that gains made in one dimension of the employment relation can not only be offset by losses in another but can be overwhelmed by those losses. And whether or not this happens depends entirely on the contingent and exogenously determined balance between capital and labor. It cannot be predicted on the basis of economic growth alone, as Gramsci's theory would require.

Now, this is not to deny a connection between economic dynamism and workers' consent. There is little doubt that, everything else being equal, it is easier to achieve industrial peace in a dynamic economy than a stagnant one. But even in these conditions, the generation of consent is uneven in scope and always very precarious. It is under constant pressure, always in danger of being undermined by the aspects of the wage relation that continue to impose harm or may even be intensified as a part of the very process developing the productive forces. What we can reliably suppose is that the *incidence* of consent among the laboring classes is greater under conditions of growth, but for it to become the *dominant* orientation is a far more difficult task.

Does Stability Depend on Consent Anyway?

A second and more fundamental problem with the Gramscian argument is this: even if a growing economy were enough to elicit *consent*, it is not clear that this is the fundamental source of capitalist *stability* anyway. The simplest test of the argument from consent is to ask: what happens when the conditions that sustain it are absent? Gramsci's argument rests on the proposition that dominant classes can continue to secure the laboring class's consent as long as they can deliver increases in living standards. But what happens when these increases are not in the offing? What happens if capitalism sinks into a period of stagnation in working-class life chances? Such a situation should have a direct impact on the acquisition of consent, which, in turn, should undermine the political status quo.

This is more or less what Gramsci, and most of his contemporaries, seemed to believe. When capitalism loses its dynamism, and the growth of the social surplus slows down, it was expected to intensify conflict over income distribution. The ruling class would be unable to coordinate its own interests with those of the subordinate classes because it would not be able to show that everyone benefited from its economic domination. What was a positive-sum game between the classes in a healthy economy would take on more of a negative-sum character. This would lead eventually to a breakdown of consent. And that, turn, would destabilize the system. In these conditions, capitalists would have no choice but to rely increasingly on *coercion* to maintain their rule. Whether in the workplace or in society more generally, force would come to replace persuasion as the basis of class dominance.

Thus, Gramsci describes political rule as "hegemony backed by the armour of coercion."[32] More elaborately, when hegemony breaks down, the ideological hold of the dominant classes over subordinate groups begins to break down. The important point is that in his theory, the political space opened up by the ebbing of consent is filled in by coercion:

> If the ruling class has lost its consensus, i.e. is no longer "leading" but only "dominant", exercising coercive force alone, this means precisely that the great masses have become detached from their traditional ideologies, and no longer believe what they used to believe previously.[33]

But why should *coercion* be the response to the dilution of consent? The answer, again, came from Marx's 1859 preface. The erosion of consent is a response to the onset of economic stagnation, and the latter is the signal that the dominant class has ceased to play its progressive role. These are the conditions under which an emerging class, promising a new economic system, is expected to make its bid for power. Its economic dynamism is supposed to enable it to cobble together a bloc of classes, and then, upon taking power, it should oversee a new era of economic growth, which, in turn, will elicit the "spontaneous" consent of the masses. In short, the erosion of consent is the harbinger of a systemic crisis and, on its back, an era of revolution. Having lost its grip over the masses, the dominant class has to fend off the inevitable challenge to its rule, for which it resorts to coercion. The loss of one is balanced by reliance on the other.

But what Gramsci never adequately considered was this—what if consent erodes but the expected challenge to the dominant class fails to materialize? What if the stagnation continued but the subordinate classes, which were expected to coalesce into a revolutionary coalition, remained subdued or unable to cohere as a political force? He was certainly aware of this possibility, as were his peers in the socialist movement. But while they were able to consider it as a possibility, they believed it could not be sustained for very long. Sooner or later, there would have to be a resolution: either the emerging classes would find a way to overcome their paralysis or the dominant class would consolidate its rule—by force, if necessary. Hence, while they acknowledged its possibility, and even designed a preliminary vocabulary to conceptualize it, they never generated a theory to understand its dynamics.[34]

The inattentiveness to this question was, of course, somewhat understandable. After all, this was a generation that took itself to be in the midst of the very revolutionary era Marx's theory predicted. The dominant class's loss of prestige had led to a political juncture in which the subordinate classes were making a bid for power, and consent was, in fact, being displaced by coercion, evidenced most sharply in the rise of fascism. But the experience of the neoliberal era in postwar capitalism has been very different and calls for a more careful consideration of the theory. It is very difficult to make sense of capitalism's continued stability on the basis of a Gramscian theory, at least in the form we have inherited it.

The salient fact about capitalism in the neoliberal era is that it has coincided with a persistent stagnation in living standards for the subordinate classes. And this is true across the advanced economies, albeit in varying degrees and for unequal durations of time. In the United States, wage growth has been close to zero for two generations, and in Germany and Great Britain, for close to two decades.[35] Yet, even as living standards have suffered and conditions of work have deteriorated, there has barely been a ripple in the political waters. By conventional measures, working-class resistance has grown weaker, even as employment conditions have worsened. Strike activity in the United States declined almost in tandem with stagnating wages so that, by the ascension of Donald Trump in 2016, it had not seen a significant uptick in three decades. So too in Britain; the last great labor upsurge was in the mid-1980s and ended in a defeat from which the unions have not recovered.

Even stagnating living standards have not triggered the kind of labor mobilization hegemony theorists might have predicted. But on many indicators, even as labor has remained quiescent, the degree of active consent to the social order has continued to decline. To the extent that public opinion polls are a reliable marker, working people are deeply dissatisfied with the status quo and, in particular, the widening gap between asset holders and the general population. How, then, might we explain the continued stability of the system if the conditions that generate its primary anchor—the consent of the working class—have significantly weakened? On Gramsci's own account, the erosion of consent should have led to political instability.[36]

Might we suppose that the masses' consent is not the foundation on which the dominant class's rule rests?

3.5
From Consent to Resignation

The argument from cultural hegemony is, as we have seen, questionable on two grounds: first, in its supposition that an improvement along one dimension of working-class experience can neutralize the perception of harms along others; second, in its refusal to countenance the possibility that consent might substantially diminish without the system falling into crisis. Together, these factors cast serious doubt about the argument, even in its materialist version. A theory of capitalist stability cannot take consent to be the bedrock upon which it rests.

A more plausible explanation for capitalism's political stability locates it not in the working class embracing its situation but in *resigning* itself to it—that is, workers accept their location in the class structure because they see no other viable option. Consent would be crucial as the anchor for political stability if, at all times, workers had a viable exit option. If they had the freedom to opt out of capitalism, eliciting their consent to the current system would be the only reliable mechanism for maintaining it. There are two ways they might choose to exit the system. The first is if they had the ability to leave the labor market. If every employee could freely choose between work and nonwork, employment contracts would have to be changed to better reflect their interests, rather than favoring the interests of employers. This would, in turn, allow that if they chose to work, it would be because they wanted to, not because they had to. But as I argued in Chapter 1, the actual inducement to work comes from the fact that workers, in fact, do *not* have the option of choosing nonwork. They participate in wage labor, not because they see it as an intrinsically desirable social relation but because their structural situation *compels* them to sell their labor power.

The second way workers might opt out is via the route predicted by Marx and his early followers—changing the system through collective action. But as I argued in Chapter 2, this argument drastically underestimates the obstacles to class formation. Capitalism not only distributes productive assets unequally but, in consequence, also generates an unequal distribution of class capacities. At the heart of the asymmetry is the fact that workers have to organize themselves to advance their interests, while a capitalist can typically advance his interests without having to coordinate with his peers. This, of course, places all the normal burdens of collective action on workers—burdens that early Marxists never adequately theorized. And, on the other side, their class rivals are relieved of that very responsibility, since the typical capitalist is able to protect his interests in his relation with his employees without having to organize with other capitalists. But equally, since he does not have to expend his resources on forging class organizations, the capitalist has the freedom to expend them on preventing, or breaking up, the organizations built by his employees—if they manage to cobble them together at all.

So workers are disadvantaged in the political contest on two distinct levels—facing greater obstacles to collective action ceteris paribus and, on top of that, having to defend against the disruptive strategies of their employers, which heaps on an additional layer of difficulties. Hence, I concluded in Chapter 2, workers will rationally choose an individualized mode of resistance over a collective one—if they resist at all. They can only begin to wage class struggle when they manage to overcome the obstacles to collective action.

This is to say that workers do not have a viable exit option in the normal course of events. They can neither opt out of their structural location nor overthrow it as and when they desire. They consent to capitalism because they see no other option as a means of sustaining themselves. Hence, the dominant class does not have to depend on workers' active consent to the system. Of course, they will benefit from it *if* it is forthcoming. A class that manages to increase the incidence of consent within the working population will be more secure in its dominance. But this is not the foundation for the system's reproduction. The more fundamental mechanism, the one that remains in place even when consent breaks down and keeps workers coming back to their job every day—and thereby reproducing the system—is what Marx called "the dull compulsion of economic relations."

This does not mean working-class consent plays no role in the reproduction of capitalism. It suggests that its spread within the class is always ephemeral because it is linked to conditions that are themselves unstable. In periods of steady growth, in which there are also mechanisms that translate productivity increases into income gains, there will be a greater spread of active consent to the system. This is something like what occurred in the decades immediately after World War II, when capitalism experienced it most rapid growth, and, on its back, so did working-class incomes. This was the era of consent, if ever there was one. But with the onset of slower growth and wage stagnation, which was in full swing by the 1980s, capitalism entered a new era. The institutions that had enabled a political exchange between labor and capital were slowly dismantled, and the income gains from production went overwhelmingly to capitalists and managers. In this period, it was neither consent nor coercion that maintained the status quo but the overwhelming pressure, imposed on the general population, of economic survival. There is a rich literature now on the culture of neoliberalism—the atomization, the sense of helplessness, the erosion of social bonds, the retreat inward. All these were symptoms of the same underlying condition—namely, that the source for social stability had shifted powerfully toward resignation.

Hence, a high-growth capitalism will have a greater degree of consent within the working class than a low-growth one, and a capitalism with a working class sufficiently organized to effectuate a political exchange with employers will have a greater propensity for consensus than one in which it is unorganized. And one with neither will fall back on resignation alone. When the class is organized and the normal sources of consent break down, and the feeling of resignation is overcome, the Marxian scenario of a revolutionary transition becomes a political option. Stability is thus governed by the interaction of economic growth and political organization. Figure 3.1 summarizes the possible outcomes.

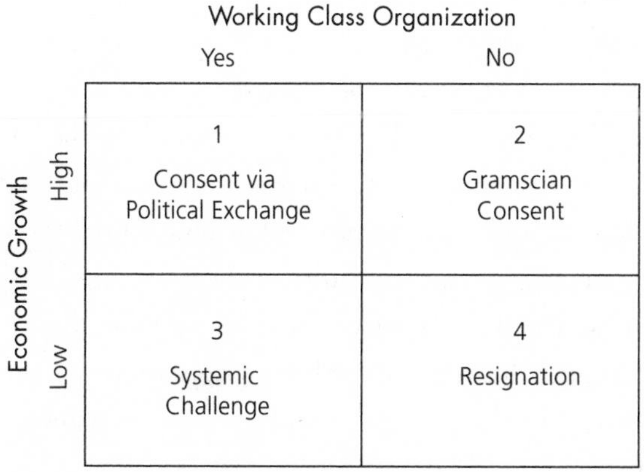

Figure 3.1 Possible Outcomes of Economic Growth and Political Organization

It bears mentioning that boxes 1 and 2 should be read as "consent overlaid atop resignation." It is not that consent ever displaces resignation altogether within the laboring classes; rather, its incidence increases. This argument flows from my observation, in Section 3.4, that the improvement of material conditions along one dimension of the employment relation cannot be assumed to ameliorate the harms generated in the other dimensions. This means that there is a baseline level of resentment that workers harbor toward their situation, springing from the class relation itself, which neither Gramscian consent, nor the more ambitious kind described by Przeworski, can dissolve. The primary source for their participation in wage labor remains the dull compulsion of economic relations. What changes is the *degree* to which this compulsion operates as a motivator.

The preceding account of capitalist stability differs from Gramsci's in that it shifts the explanation from consent to resignation. It is worth mentioning that Gramsci was certainly aware of the phenomenon. He explains in the *Notebooks* that crises sometimes can be averted when the status quo is losing legitimacy but that the masses "have either acquired the habits and customs necessary for the new systems of living and working, or else they continue to be subject to coercive pressure through the elementary necessities of their existence."[37] The reliance of "habits and customs" formed among the masses from the mundane "necessities of their existence" seems to be a gesture toward what I have described as resignation. Gramsci does seem to be alluding to the possibility of the dominant class's reliance on this phenomenon as a source of stability, rather than on consent, pure and simple. But while it makes an appearance, it remains peripheral to his broader political sociology. It is never integrated into his explanation for class dominance.

3.6

The Place of Ideology

It remains to ask what, if any, role there is for ideology in the framework I have developed. I have argued that capitalism's durability stems fundamentally from the material pressures exerted on social actors by its class structure. This is a quite stark contrast to the culturalist framework developed in the postwar decades, in which ideology was elevated to a primary role. But while I maintain that the culturalists endowed ideology with an unduly inflated role, I do not mean to argue for its irrelevance. On the contrary, ideology has to figure in any materialist account of capitalism. But as I argue in the following, its location is very different from the one assigned to it by culturalists. Whereas, in the latter framework, ideology serves as a *cause* of the structures' stabilization, in my argument, it is a *consequence* of that stabilization.

I have argued that the source of workers' consent to capitalism, to the extent that it occurs, is not ideology but the pressure of their circumstances—the choices that are, in fact, available to them by virtue of their structural location and the power relations in which they are embedded. Now, this does not mean ideology is irrelevant to the process of capitalist stabilization. It means only that it cannot be what *motivates* workers to accept their position in the structure. The motivation comes from their material interests. However, ideology still plays an important and identifiable role—as a means of *rationalization*. For both capitalists and workers, the individuals embedded in those locations have to create cultural and normative codes that enable them to subjectively apprehend their decisions. They have to generate rationalizations for *why* they accept the rules of the game.

III

Goran Therborn has suggested that a primary function of ideology is to ensure that class actors are endowed with a subjectivity that enables them to "qualify for [their] given roles" in the structure so that they "are capable of carrying them out."[38] Hence, ideology provides them with the subjective resources to carry out the strategies imposed on them by the structures.

Now, for any such theory, there is one fundamental constraint that must be observed. If, in a materialist theory, ideology is a means for actors to rationalize their location, it is bound by the same condition I imposed on the culturalist theory—it has to respect the basic cognitive abilities of the actors. The rationalization cannot, therefore, be a hallucination. The ideology must be reinforced and sanctified by the basic facts of the actors' condition, for if the ideology denied them, we must expect that it would lose its attractiveness to the actors themselves. It cannot, therefore, serve as a kind of "false consciousness"—a veil that altogether obscures the actual functioning of social structures. But rationalizations, by their nature, are not outright falsehoods—they are ways we learn to live with the facts, not a blanket denial of the facts. Hence, to construe ideology as a kind of rationalization imposes a very different analytical burden on a theory than if we supposed ideology was simply false consciousness.

In the case of the working class, we have already seen that they accept capitalist rules of the game not because they view them as legitimate or desirable but because they see no other choice. It is a small step to predict that workers' ideological reaction will be to *naturalize* the class structure. They will rationalize the pressures imposed on them as basic facts of life, much like the laws of nature—something that is unpleasant and odious but cannot be changed. This does not mean they see the system as a force standing apart from human action;

after all, they encounter it through the lived experience of the work-place and the legally sanctioned authority of the manager / owner. The stamp of human institutions is visible in every dimension of private property. But the remorseless burden of economic pressures, the enormous disparity in power between them and their employer, and the prohibitive costs of collective action—all these factors combine to give the structures an appearance of immutability.

While the naturalization of the class structure is common among workers, it also finds an echo among employers. They are, after all, highly constrained by their location, much the same as their employees. Hence, much as with workers, we should expect capitalists to take their roles as being expressions of deep, unchanging facts of human society, no more subject to manipulation than biological facts. The difference between them will be that in addition to seeing the rules of capitalism as natural laws, capitalists will also be far more likely to view them as legitimate and desirable. A materialist class theory predicts that the winners in a social system will apprehend their constraints as not merely binding but beneficial, and they will project the narrow gains that accrue to them as social gains. This is not just true of capitalism—in any social system, the dominant group should be expected to not only generate a legitimizing ideology but also internalize it more fully than any other.

Hence, perhaps ironically, the class that actively consents to capitalism is not the working class but the class that rules over it. The problem with cultural theory is not that it highlights the importance of consent but that it seeks it out in the wrong class. Whereas workers will tend to view the system as unchanging and unfair, capitalists will endorse it as a natural expression of human nature—and also desirable. This is how rationalization takes divergent forms between the two classes and reflects the difference in their constraints and their fortunes. In neither instance is it simply false consciousness. In both cases, the actors' rationalizations reflect their actual situation to a considerable extent. So, too, the content varies in accordance to the experience of each party. Whereas, for workers, we should expect their naturalizing reaction to be expressed in cynicism about the system—its being corrupt and so on—and in a general tendency to be very pessimistic about social change, among capitalists we should expect a tendency not just to naturalize capitalism but to celebrate its proximity to human nature, to see their own success as proof of its fairness, to warn against changing anything that so directly expresses deep human drives, and so forth.

Ideology thus occupies an important place in a materialist class theory. But it operates as an effect of actors' class strategies, not as a cause. In this capacity, it conforms to Marx's general dictum that it is agents' social being that determines their consciousness and not their consciousness that determines their being.

3.7

The New Left's Folly

There is a deep and abiding irony in the research program launched by the New Left in the postwar era, of which the cultural turn was the lineal descendant. Figures like Stuart Hall, some of the Frankfurt School philosophers, and cultural Gramscians understood their project to center around mending one of the deepest lacunae in classical Marxism—its eschatological view of capitalism. As the New Left and its descendants understood it, the survival and stabilization of the system were anomalous from the standpoint of the original theory. The problem, they suggested, was that the theory was overly focused on the factors that pushed the system toward collapse, to the detriment of theorizing the sources of stabilization. This was a natural consequence of the theory's promotion of the economic structure over the contribution of culture—of the "base" over the "superstructure." In order to understand how capitalism survived, critical theory would have to turn to the play of cultural institutions—the role of ideology, identity, values, and so on.

But in making this move, the postwar theorists were actually *internalizing* classical Marxism's weakness, not remedying it. They were tacitly accepting the argument that the structure was the location of capitalism's destabilizing mechanisms and that its sources of stability would therefore have to be found *outside* that structure. Like the classical Marxists, they refused to countenance the possibility that the class structure had a dual logic, which certainly created social conflict but also contained it within manageable limits. The New Left was correct in its charge that classical Marxists had paid insufficient attention to the forces that undermine class formation and thus sustain capitalism over time. But in the end, the program they launched had the same effect. In an important respect, in spite of their identification as mavericks—as theorists breaking out of orthodoxy—they operated within the foundational assumptions of the theory they were criticizing.

The argument I have offered in this chapter departs from the culturalist program in two ways. First, it suggests that the real source of capitalist stability is the class structure itself. From this follows the second and more portentous point—that far from careening toward imminent collapse, *capitalism underwrites its own stability.* This conclusion flows naturally from the premise that capitalism distributes class capacities unequally between employers and employees. If this is so, then even while it generates antagonism and conflict between them, the conflict will tend to be resolved in favor of employers. Since the path to capitalism's supersession runs through class formation, and since the odds are stacked against the latter, it follows that the system will tend to steer class antagonism toward a form that is manageable and keep its intensity within an acceptable range—thereby maintaining stable reproduction. This is built into the structure itself and is not the product of the ruling groups' cultural agency. The New Left was therefore right in thinking that classical Marxists had not adequately theorized the sources of stability in capitalism. But the problem was that the classical tradition had not developed the implications of their own theory. In failing to recognize this, and thereby seeking the resolution to the problem in the cultural domain, the postwar theorists not only were led down a dubious intellectual path but missed an opportunity to develop the very research program to which they professed fidelity.

4

Agency, Contingency, and All That

The preceding chapters have developed a quite austere structural theory of capitalism and its class processes. In many ways, it leans against the direction that social theory has taken in the recent past, wherein a baseline skepticism toward structural arguments has been the norm. Of course, I have also tried to generate an account of the conditions in which political agency can be effectuated *given* the constraints faced by subaltern groups. We thus have a theory of capitalism in which there is an interplay between structural forces on one side and the conscious, directed intervention of organized political actors on the other. To complicate matters even more, while I have developed this argument on a consistently materialist foundation, I have tried to do so while acknowledging the role of culture within both the structural and the agential dimensions of the account.

In this chapter I examine how a theory of this kind fares with regard to some of the metatheoretical concerns of the cultural turn. As explained in the introduction, the shift toward culture was in some measure motivated by a desire to affirm the role of agency in social life. Many theorists, exemplified most famously by E. P. Thompson, felt that the structuralism of their time not only ignored social agency but was incapable of giving it the recognition it deserved. The intensity and polemical ferocity with which Thompson made his case has left its mark on the debates that followed. There remains an abiding sense that structural theories cannot make sense of the way people actually navigate their lives because these theories reduce people to little more than the bearers of social structures. Since people go about like robots, obeying the commands of the system, social processes seem governed by ineluctable "laws," not conscious human action. And, of course, because agency is minimized in this fashion, while the determinism of structural reproduction is amplified, the theory seems to have little hope of acknowledging, let alone explaining, the place of *contingency* in social interaction. And this, in turn, makes structural theories incapable of acknowledging the heterogeneity and richness of social life. Structural theories flatten and homogenize the social landscape, while a focus on agency enables us to comprehend its variability.

The concerns about agency are certainly valid. Some versions of structuralism have been guilty of a kind of functionalism, thereby ignoring the questions of agency. And it is also true that they gloss over the variability of social structures. But those are more instances of a theory being poorly developed than of being a poor theory. I argue that, if properly understood, a structural class theory does not have to underplay the role of conscious choice in social reproduction; indeed, understanding the structural location of action is a crucial precondition to appreciating the content of agency. So, too, I show that, if properly calibrated, a structural class theory has the virtue of distinguishing between those aspects of social life that are, in fact, highly constrained, and thereby stable over time, and those that are beyond the influence of the class structure. In other words, the virtue of structural theory is that it enables us to appreciate contingency or variability where it occurs, rather than treating it as a necessary feature of all social interaction.

4.1

A Reprise

The argument developed in the preceding chapters assigns some very powerful properties to the class structure. It suggests that once the structure is in place—once it has, in fact, displaced antediluvian economic systems—it imposes a very stringent choice set on the actors who inhabit it. On one side, owners are constrained to pursue a cost-minimizing, profit-maximizing growth strategy in order to survive in the market; on the other, workers are compelled to offer their labor services to these establishments and do what they can to hold on to their jobs. These compulsions hold regardless of culture and geography, as do the responses to them. Far from being limited by the local meaning universe, the class structure works by subordinating the local culture to its own demands. Two implications, in particular, are worth drawing out.

First, the argument is able to explain how it happens that capitalism generates broadly similar economic dynamics wherever it takes root. The micro-level pressures generate responses that aggregate as system-wide patterns of behavior—captured evocatively by Marx as capitalism's "laws of motion" and in today's lexicon as "macrodynamics." The theory thus explains how the class structure is responsible for generating distinctively capitalist macrodynamics, compared to the dynamics of state socialist systems or older, precapitalist ones.

Of course, just what those dynamics are can still be under contention. Neoclassical economists may disagree with those working in
a Schumpetarian or Marxist tradition. But what most current economic frameworks agree upon is that whatever the system-wide economic patterns are, they stem from the profit-maximizing behavior
of firms and workers' defense of their material well-being. In that
respect, the theory recovers the foundations for a genuine political
economy of capitalism, in spite of the cultural turn.

Second, the theory suggests that the class structure itself underwrites capitalism's stability. This is where my argument is furthest
from early Marxists and the cultural turn. Early Marxists had been
aware of the stability-inducing properties of the class structure but
never adequately theorized it. They focused, instead, on the myriad
ways class domination generated social conflict, thus reinforcing the
message of *The Communist Manifesto* that the system tended toward
its own demise. The New Left took this conclusion as the premise
for its own work and turned, wrongly, to culture as the reason the
demise had been forestalled. My argument suggests that the main
source for capitalism's stability is the class structure itself. Once the
workforce is proletarianized, and once its members have to seek out
employment in order to survive, they consent to the system, not because of the power of ideology but because of what Marx called the
"dull compulsion of economic relations." This compulsion not only
inserts them into the employment relation but inclines them to opt
for individualized bargaining strategies over collective ones. But the
very act of opting for individual strategies ends up reproducing the
domination of the employer since, as Adam Smith noted, in a one-
on-one standoff, the employer wins. It is only when all the obstacles
to collective action are overcome that workers can resist as a class—

and that is the exception, not the norm. Hence, the system tends toward political stability, not revolution.

4.2

Agents and Automatons

An argument of this kind is sure to set off alarm bells. And it should. In the recent past, theorists have become quite suspicious of theories that place such a strong emphasis on structural forces. The fundamental problem is ably expressed by William Sewell:

> Structures tend to appear in social scientific discourse as impervious to human agency, to exist apart from, but nevertheless to determine the essential shape of, the strivings and motivated transactions that constitute the experienced surface of social life. A social science trapped in an unexamined metaphor of structure tends to reduce actors to cleverly programmed automatons.[1]

Several examples bearing out Sewell's concerns come to mind. The most obvious is, of course, Talcott Parson's structural functionalism. In a Parsonian world, structures persist because of their functionality for the wider system, and actors are socialized into their roles, which they accept more or less automatically. On the other side of the spectrum is Louis Althusser's Marxian brand of structuralism, in which he describes his actors as *trager*—quite literally, as *supports* of social structures. Now, in Althusser's defense, his characterization of economic actors as *trager* is meant to be a description of how they appear in Marx's *Capital*. And, to some extent, he is right. In the first volume of Marx's great work, the presentation of argument often resorts to a kind of Hegelian language in which the structures seem to have minds of their own. The clearest instance of this is when Marx describes capital as "self-valorizing," as if capital itself has intentionality.[2] But while this is true of his presentation, it is not true of the structure of the argument itself, which is easy to explicate in causal terms, even if Marx himself does not always succeed in doing so. In Althusser's work, however, this shortcoming is trumpeted as a virtue and the rhetorical flaws of Marx's argument are turned into explanatory principles. Hence, whatever one thinks of the substance of E. P. Thompson's furious response in *The Poverty of Theory*, his consternation with Althusser's framework is easy to fathom. Structures, for the French Marxist, do seem to have mystical powers. So there is ample precedent for the charge that structural theories bury social agency. The question is, *must* they?

Agency is a concept used to describe one way humans intervene in the world around them. It is distinguished by the fact that it is an intervention motivated by *reasons*—as opposed to animal instinct or pure habit. To invoke agency as the factor behind a social outcome is to suggest that the outcome was not only the product of human intervention but intervention motivated by a set of goals. Now, it is quite possible that the outcome actually generated was not what was intended—unintended consequences are entirely compatible with a robust conception of agency. In such cases, the analyst would be encouraged to explain how the chain of events triggered by agential intervention took a turn different from the one intended. But whether intended or not, the recognition of agency requires, at its core, that we connect actors' actions to the motivating reasons.[3]

This being the case, a structural theory does not have to suppress the role of social agency. The challenge is to show how structures are involved in generating reasons for the actions in question. In other words, structures can be causally relevant, not because they turn actors into automatons but because they have an impact on the actors' reasoning about *how* to intervene in the world. They can perform this function because they are part of the constraints actors have to account for as they engage the world around them. Those constraints make it attractive to pursue one course of action rather than another because of the consequences they are able to impose on the individuals embedded within the structure. If we can show that actors choose to intervene in the way they do because of the impact of the structures—hence showing that they matter because the actors acknowledge their impact on their reasoning—it is not a suppression of their agency. To the contrary, it is a fuller account of how agency unfolds in a world of constraints.

Consider how this is in evidence in my account of the class structure. I suggest that, once it is in place, it tends toward stability, not implosion. The class structure tends to reproduce itself. This certainly sounds as if we are back to a Parsonian world of systems calling into being the conditions needed to sustain themselves. But the logic of my argument is quite different. The structure is not reproduced because it turns agents into automatons but because it generates good *reasons* for them to play by its rules. The capitalist class structure generates a set of options for workers regarding their economic welfare. They can choose to either submit to the labor market or reject it. But the choices come with consequences. Workers enter the labor market, and submit to an employer's authority, because they deem it unwise to choose the other option. In a Parsonian world, actors pursue their course of action either because their socialization impels them to do so or because the functional requirements of the system have the power to substitute for agential reasoning. But that is not what is happening here. In the argument I have developed, actors pursue their strategies even if their socialization enjoins them to reject it because they are actively weighing the options open to them.

If it were the case that actors acceded to the structures' demands because they lacked agency, the system would actually be vulnerable to breakdown. Suppose workers accept employer authority because, as automatons, they are directed to by their "programming." They follow the rules, or do what they're told, because they naively believe what dominant groups tell them about the world. If this were so, it would simply be a matter of explaining to them what the situation actually is—how they are being harmed by their structural situation, how it will benefit them to generate organizations for collective action, that they will flourish within an alternative system, and so on. This might take some time, of course, because a lifetime of propaganda cannot be neutralized overnight. They might be skeptical at first, even dismissive. But, over time, having explained the situation to them and thereby enabling them to acquire a better sense of the harms they are undergoing, we will have restored the conditions for effective agency. They will now have the ability to consider the option of resisting the demands of the structures. And since, on assumption, the reason they submit to the structures is *not* because they have weighed their options but because of their having internalized their assigned roles, there is a high probability that they will now, having learned the truth, refuse to do what has hitherto been expected of them. They will be very likely to undertake the organized resistance needed to substantially improve their situation.

But, in fact, as I argued in Chapter 2, employees virtually never agree to take up collective action simply because someone explains to them the harms of employer power. The reason they hesitate is not because they are automatons but because they have a fairly accurate understanding of their economic vulnerability. And this inclines them to proceed with caution. They will tend to prioritize individualistic strategies over collective ones because, even though a successful collective campaign will likely generate more benefits than an individual one, the risk / cost matrix associated with building the former is, in most situations, prohibitive. In other words, they obey the rules because the class structure generates good reasons for them to do so. They submit knowingly, aware of the harms associated with their situation but wary of the potential for even greater harm if they risk challenging their employer. This is why labor organizing is such an arduous process—precisely because employees are *not* blindly following the rules. This is why it takes a great deal of backbreaking work to create the culture of resistance, trust and commitment, and steely determination required to challenge employer power in capitalism. It is because workers have good reason to respect the constraints under which they subsist.

Two important conclusions follow from this. First, it turns out that our choice is not just between structural theories and voluntarist ones but also between *two kinds* of *structural* theories—functionalist versus casual. When he accuses structural theories of suppressing human agency, Sewell is unduly restricting the options to just one of the possible varieties of structural analysis. His objections only make sense if we assume that all such theories must be functionalist in form. And, indeed, if that were the case, his injunction against the approach would be justified. But once we see that structural accounts can also be formulated in a causal language, the worries turn out to be misplaced. Indeed, where actors are, in fact, structurally constrained, such that they formulate their strategies in order to navigate those constraints, a structural theory does not *efface* agency so much as it helps us *understand* it.

Second, this analysis enables us to also recast the relationship between determinism and agency in a somewhat startling fashion. We have seen that capitalism's remarkable stability issues from that fact that actors accept their location in the structure knowingly, not as automatons. But this is another way of saying that a process that is quite deterministic—the steady, predictable reproduction of a social relation over time—is the product of fully activated social agency. Every day, workers get up and go to their jobs, actively seek out jobs, or search for ways to move up the job ladder, while their employers seek to deploy their labor, market their products, compete against rivals, and so on. They do this because it makes sense for them given their constraints and needs. And all these activities require enormous drive, creativity, imagination, and resolve—qualities that are essential ingredients of agency. There is nothing automatic or passive about seeking out and finding a job, or holding on to one in competitive conditions, or marketing a product and winning out in the warlike domain of the product market. And this means, in turn, that a structural process, which is quite deterministic in its outcome, is generated by the active intervention of social agency.

Once we allow that structures depend on conscious agency, it frees us of the worry that we must, as a rule, be suspicious of deterministic arguments in order to respect agency. Structural and deterministic theories are fully compatible with conscious human choice. And if this is so, we can reject the glib association—virtually an orthodoxy in current debates—between agency and contingency. Agency can be taken to be present in both kinds of processes, deterministic and contingent; where they differ will be in how conscious actions are connected to the background conditions. In the case of deterministic explanations, the background conditions will be part of the explanation for the action because they in some measure motivated the actor to undertake the course of action we are examining. But where those conditions do not exercise a causal influence on his action, we can deem the latter *contingent* with respect to those conditions—they are causally irrelevant to his interventions, hence making the latter contingent with respect to the former. Both are instances of agency—in one case occurring because agents see good reason to undertake structurally constrained courses of action and, in the other, because they are motivated by reasons not connected to the structures. Hence, instead of dismissing determinism out of hand, we are obliged to treat it as an empirical matter—to examine whether the outcomes we are examining are, in fact, deterministic or not, for surely many social processes are. And if we resolve that they are, we can then analyze how the structures produce these deterministic outcomes by generating the reasons that incline actors to choose the predicted course of action.

4.3
Too Little Contingency?

In this section we explore more carefully how a structural class theory can accommodate the fact of social contingency. It is quite common to encounter the charge that this is precisely what it cannot do. The language in which this criticism is expressed varies depending on the theoretical tradition, but because of the influence of post-structuralism, the most common recent practice is to lean on the idiom associated with it. Hence, we find arguments that "grand narratives"—structural theories of social change or reproduction—illicitly homogenize the social landscape. As Dipesh Chakrabarty puts it, they ignore the "heterogeneities and incommensurabilities" of social life.[4] The basic idea is that these grand narratives tend to assume structures have so much power that they leave no room for the persistence of social difference, local and regional particularities, variety across cultures, and so on. Everything flows from the structure, and nothing is allowed to deviate from its logic; its causal force simply homogenizes the social landscape. Insofar as there is some variation, it is assumed to be temporary, so that, if we wait long enough, those recalcitrant social practices, still enjoying some independence from the structure's gravitational pull, will be subsumed under it soon enough.[5]

The criticism from heterogeneity is a call to appreciate the contingencies of social life. It is a warning that any theory that describes the gamut of social institutions as being determined by one, or even a cluster, of structural forces is not likely to survive scrutiny. And the critics are surely justified in their admonishments against such "totalizing narratives." It is self-evident that, in spite of capitalism's spread across the world, it has not dissolved national cultures. While theorists often focus on the convergence of social practices along many dimensions, it remains the case that there are recognizable differences in the way the economies and the broader culture is organized from country to country and across regions within countries. The question for us is as follows: is a structural class theory, of the kind I defend, capable of appreciating the persistence of social heterogeneity, or must it commit to a totalizing narrative in which the juggernaut of a globalizing capitalism swallows up and homogenizes entire regions and cultures?

Heterogeneity from Without

Looking at the history of structural class theory, there would seem to be ample reason for concern. Consider the base-superstructure model central to classical Marxism. It is a quite common interpretation that economic relations belong to the base—and everything else to the superstructure. And since the base is said to determine the superstructure, it amounts to claiming that the economy determines everything that is noneconomic. And if that is so, it reduces social contingency to irrelevance. The economic base is understood as precisely that juggernaut that so worries critics—rolling over all other social relations and subsuming them under its own logic. Not surprisingly, most elaborations of the theory in the postwar era have struggled to reduce the theory's ambition since the baseline claims are obviously unsustainable.[6]

But a structural class theory does not have to be so implausible in its claims. It does not have to commit to being a "totalizing" theory. Recall the discussion in Chapter 1. I argued there that the class structure operates through culture but is nevertheless independent of it. What this means is that, once the class structure is in place, its reproduction will not be imperiled by agents potentially failing to understand its demands. They do have to interpret what it means to be wage laborers or capitalists. But the interpretive work required of them is so minimal that it is virtually assured of success. No wage laborer fails to understand what he needs to do to seek out and maintain employment, and capitalists very quickly pick up what they need to do if they want to stay afloat. And in the event that their socialization inhibits them from accepting its demands, they will have good reason to adjust their normative stance so it accommodates their practice, as long as they are actually embedded in the structure. Wage laborers repelled by the demands of the labor market will have to adjust to it anyway, unless they find alternative means of income—but in that case, they are no longer wage laborers. So as long as they are, in fact, wage laborers, they will, however grudgingly, have to accommodate to its demands, whatever their normative codes tell them. Of course, they will find various ways of resisting the terms of the employment relation. But that is a conflict *within* the structure; it presumes their participation in it, and hence their acquiescence to its basic rules, even if they strive to improve their situation within it. And so, too, with capitalists.

It might seem that this is an argument for capitalism homogenizing the surrounding culture, as postcolonial critics charge. My claim seems to be that capitalism, as it spreads, finds an endless variety of cultures but then subordinates them to its own logic. And this seems to be a way of resurrecting the classical Marxian claim about the economy determining the content of noneconomic institutions. But I am making a less ambitious claim—for the class structure being *independent* of culture but not *determinative* of it. This does require of it the power to overturn some aspects of the surrounding culture—but not all of them. It only requires that class structure transform and subordinate those components of actors' meaning orientation that block or interfere with their ability to participate in it.

Consider again the example of a recently proletarianized wage laborer. He has been born with a particular worldview, he observes certain religious practices, he has his culinary preferences, he observes particular norms of comportment with his peers, and so on. These will reflect the wider culture into which he is born, and this culture will differ from region to region. Now suppose that he is thrown into the labor market and forced to seek employment to sustain himself. Nothing in the theory I have offered demands that his *entire* outlook and symbolic universe be rewritten in the same codes as that of a worker in Manchester or Detroit—as implied in the idea that the class structure determines culture in toto and, in so doing, tends to homogenize cultures. All it predicts is that he will adjust those components of his culture that interfere with his ability to hold on to his job: perhaps some part of his religious beliefs, social routine, sleeping habits, or so on. The *rest* of his habits, norms, and expectations can remain untouched. So, too, with the capitalist. The only components of his symbolic universe that will feel pressure are implicated in his ability to manage labor and turn a profit. As we scale upward and consider the implications for the region as a whole, it means that many parts of its broader culture may not feel a pressure to change and might continue as they are.

Notice that this explication of the relation between structure and contingency is entirely in line with my argument in the final paragraph of the preceding section. I suggested there that, if properly conceptualized, determinism and contingency are both instances of social agency. Where they differ is that, in one instance, the structure generates reasons for actors to follow regular and repeated actions, aggregating into social patterns; in the other instance, the structure does not generate similar reasons for action, thereby making it difficult to predict what sort of action the agent will undertake and hence making the action contingent with respect to the structure. So being a worker will incline the actor in that location to make certain choices in a highly predictable and regular fashion—like seeking out employment and trying to hold on to it—but will not generate similarly compelling reasons in other domains, like which religious beliefs to hold on to while he seeks out employment. The class structure has a deterministic relation to the former set of actions but a quite contingent one with respect to the latter. But both the choices are instances of agency.

This suggests, in turn, that the imposition of capitalist relations can leave considerable swathes of local culture unchanged. Many aspects of local religion will continue as before; social mores that are not implicated in economic reproduction will remain in place; legal doctrine attending to myriad practices will continue as before, as long as it does not impede economic reproduction.

And it follows that, even as capitalism spreads across the world, it can support tremendous social diversity. We can sustain a sweeping "grand narrative" of capitalism's spread and its internal tendencies—its macrodynamics and the social antagonisms it unleashes—without projecting onto it a totalizing drive. Nations can be fully capitalist but still have substantial cultural differences. There can also be enormous regional diversity *within* a nation if state formation occurred across a very heterogeneous social landscape. It becomes entirely possible for a nation-state to become absorbed into capitalist economic relations but sustain numerous local cultures, rituals, political institutions, and so forth, just as these differences persist across nations. Just how much of the political and cultural matrix will have to change now becomes a more contingent matter, which will depend on the way these institutions interact with, and impinge upon, the demands of the class structure. Some regions might undergo a revolution in their inherited cultural practices while others will have to make only minor adjustments.

This account of the relation between the class structure and other, noneconomic institutions is substantially less ambitious than that of classical Marxism. The idea for a more restricted set of claims for the class structure's transformative power was pioneered by G. A. Cohen in his classic work on Marx's theory of history. Cohen contrasted two versions of historical materialism—the traditional, ambitious kind, which claimed extensive causal dominance of the economic base, and a more cautious one, which posited only that the base transforms those aspects of the surrounding institutions that interfere with it. This latter version he called *restricted historical materialism.*[7] The view of the class structure I defend can be taken as an elaboration of that theory. It differs in only a couple of ways.

First, it clarifies the microfoundations for the theory. While Cohen stakes a claim that the economic logic of class selects against recalcitrant institutions, he is not entirely clear as to selection mechanism.

He predicts that ideas that interfere with the development of the productive forces will be selected against while those that are consistent with ongoing development will be sustained. But he does not explain how this selection occurs. This is in keeping with Cohen's view of functional explanation—namely, that it is a viable explanatory strategy even if it does not explain how a particular functional relation between two phenomena is sustained. The explication of a mechanism helps fill out the explanation, but it is not essential for its viability. The argument I offer does provide a mechanism—it is the class actors trying to maintain their economic viability, as dictated by the structure. Of course, this is entirely consistent with Cohen's argument, since he clearly presumes that actors are not only rational in a minimal, formal sense but also substantively in that they seek to improve their welfare.[8]

Second, and perhaps more importantly, my account is agnostic about the macroeconomic effects of the selection process. For Cohen, the components of culture being selected against are those that impede growth. This is a claim about the effects of ideas on economic productivity. In his account, the components of culture that make it through the selection process are supposed to be those friendly to the continued development of the productive forces, while the ones filtered out are those that would be hostile to economic development. My argument bases the survival of ideas not on their positive effect on the productive forces' development but on the economic viability of individual class actors. The difference between the two is this: actors can defend their individual economic position without having a positive impact on aggregate social productivity. Indeed, they can do it at the expense of the latter. In feudal class structures, for example, lords were able to sustain their individual economic position even as the productive forces stagnated for decades at a time. So the selection is not against ideas that impede *societal* economic welfare but the welfare of *individual* class actors. And individual class actors have often, for long periods, maintained their position with no positive spillovers.[9]

Heterogeneity from Within

The argument so far has placed the source of social heterogeneity in noneconomic institutions. Differences between capitalist regions emanate from the persistence of ideas and practices that are beyond the reach of the economic logic of the class structure. In other words, diversity comes from phenomena that are causally independent of class. One way to express this idea is through the concept of exogeneity. Scientists often describe phenomena that are beyond the influence of a causal dynamic as being *exogenous* to that dynamic; conversely, phenomena that are constrained or influenced in some way by those causes are described as being *endogenous* to it. So, reverting to this nomenclature, one source of diversity in capitalism comes from the fact that the forces that shape many social phenomena are exogenous to the dynamics of the class structure. They are beyond its reach, and, hence, their story is contingent with respect to its own evolution.

This is not to say that the institutions outside the influence of the class structure have no causal history of their own. These phenomena—norms, political institutions, and aesthetic preferences—are shaped by a range of factors. It's just that class is not one of them. The scope of influence of economic structures is thus limited, and part of the research program of class analysis is to investigate the actual boundaries of that influence. How far does it extend into the political or ideological institutions of society? Which components does it subordinate to its logic? Those that remain outside its scope will have causal histories of their own. They are not *un*determined—they are just not determined by the class structure. Or, to put it differently, they are not purely contingent, they are just contingent with respect to the class structure. Hence, there will be other research agendas that seek to explain how those institutions evolved by tracing their own causal histories, much of which will turn out to be independent of economic forces.

This seems to suggest that the degree of social diversity in capitalist societies depends on how many factors operate exogenously to the class structure. And this would imply that what is *endogenous* to the latter is relatively homogenous—that there is a high degree of institutional and cultural convergence *within* the economic foundation of society. Everything linked to economic practice would tend to gravitate toward the same form, and those things that remain beyond its reach would persist in their diverse glory. We would expect, then, that in every region, economic institutions and those institutions that orbit around them would be quite similar in form and content, and, as we extended outward to institutions that are exogenous to the economic system, we would find a wide array of social practices operating under diverse logics.

But this proposal is misleading. To relegate all diversity to zones that are exogenous to the economic sphere radically underestimates the space for diversity *within* the economy. How is diversity possible when economic actors face the same structural pressure to increase their competitiveness, whether as sellers of labor services or as purveyors of produced commodities?

The capitalist class structure imposes on its incumbents a pressure to perform. In the case of firms, for example, it demands that they adopt cost-minimizing strategies to effectively compete in the market. But *how* they do it is not singularly determined by the market. The organization of the market and those institutions that directly impinge on it can vary enormously. So, for example, there can be a diversity in occupational structure—a capitalist economy can be predominantly agrarian or industrial; it can be dominated by services or by manufacturing; manufacturing can be dominated by small firms, as Britain was throughout the nineteenth century, or heavy industry, as Germany was from the late nineteenth century into the mid-twentieth. Labor markets can vary along several dimensions. In countries of the Global South, one observes the enormous weight of informal employment, whereas in advanced industrial countries, more durable, formal employment contracts still dominate; within the advanced world, the organization of formal employment varies tremendously, with the highly unionized and regulated Nordic countries on one extreme and the United States, where more than 90 percent of the private sector is nonunion, on the other.

This is all heterogeneity within the economic structure. And it is not trivial. It points to the fact that capitalism as an economic system can be organized along very different lines, with highly variable combinations of occupational and production patterns. These variations in its organization, in turn, generate highly divergent conditions for social and economic reproduction for its incumbents. A capitalism dominated by small firms, informal labor markets, and very low levels of labor organization will pose very different challenges for improving general welfare than a capitalism that houses large, high-productivity enterprises and high levels of union density. Whereas, in the former, one would expect to find a lower ceiling on wages, a wider scope for managerial discretion, and less input from labor in economic and political affairs, we would expect to find a contrast on those very dimensions in the latter—more scope for rising wages, greater constraints on employer authority, and greater influence for labor in the policy sphere.

Hence, there are two sources of enduring diversity and heterogeneity in capitalism: the range of phenomena that remain exogenous to the class structure and those whose variation occurs in spite of being endogenous to it. The difference between the two is that while the former are causally *independent* of class, the latter are still in some way *constrained* by it. This means that the variation of the latter kind differs from the former in that it occurs within limits set by the class structure itself. It is a limit of functional compatibility. Phenomena that impinge directly on the economic dynamics of class are pressured to conform to its requirements. And as I argued in the preceding section, the pressure comes from the individual economic strategies of the class actors themselves. But all the actors need is for the institutions to be *consistent* with their economic goals; as long as a range of institutions can serve that purpose, there is room for variation in their content. I explore this in more detail in Section 4.5.

Considering the two sources together, we can discern how misled is the boilerplate criticism, coming mostly from post-structuralist theory but also from other quarters, that a structural class theory—a "grand narrative"—cannot account for diversity. Actually, the more compelling worry comes from the other side. Over the past two decades, some theorists have wondered if the concept has much analytical traction at all, given the enormous diversity of institutional configurations compatible with capitalism. The classical Marxists, for example, once held the view that there was a deep tension between capitalism's profit-maximizing imperative and the egalitarian goals of the labor movement. But the experience of the postwar decades seemed to show that egalitarian institutions—such as those of the social democratic states in western Europe—were quite compatible with capitalism. If this is so, we have a system that not only allows for institutional variation but is so permissive as to be constraining in name only. As Fred Block queried, is there any point in retaining the concept at all?[10]

4.4

Too Much Contingency?

Not all instances of diversity are a challenge for a structural class theory. I have tried to show that, if properly understood, the theory has a quite clearly delimited zone of causal determination. It not only is able to accommodate the fact that many phenomena are beyond its influence but insists on it. The kinds of diversity that pose a potential problem are those that appear to run directly against the imperatives that, according to the theory, drive the system. Egalitarian institutions are potentially anomalous for this reason. By egalitarian, I mean two things—arrangements that reduce the inequality of income and wealth and those that reduce the inequality of power. Hence, they are equalizing in a very broad sense. A system premised on deep inequalities on both of these axes, and which is supposed to impose strict limits on the degree to which the institutions within it can diverge from its core imperatives, should screen out any significant impulse in *this* direction, even if it is happy to accommodate shifts in directions that are neutral on the score.

For this reason, the emergence of social democratic institutions in postwar Europe poses something of a challenge to structural class theory. First of all, the institutions constructed under its aegis did substantially mitigate the material inequalities generated by an unregulated capitalism. The Nordic countries, for example, seem to be on an entirely different plane than the United States, which has the most anemic redistributive thrust of any advanced industrial country. On a large variety of dimensions, the Nordic social democracies rolled back not only the economic inequalities of an unregulated capitalism but also made enormous advances in reducing the labor market insecurities associated with it. And just as importantly, they dramatically reduced the unilateral power of employers in the workplace. Employers were forced to negotiate with labor unions over a range of decisions over which they once had complete authority—wages, pensions, work hours, hiring and firing, and even investment decisions.[11] These changes were not just a permutation capitalists stumbled upon as they sought to maximize profits. They were not innovations promoted by capitalists to further their economic interests. They were, in fact, dramatic ruptures in the economic logic of the system. Their emergence required steering capitalist markets in a direction they would have never have taken otherwise.

Second, social democratic capitalisms also turned out to be highly *profitable* for capitalists. On most every measure of growth in capitalism, social democratic systems did as well or better than the more free-market system of the United States. If we look at productivity, per capita income, aggregate profitability, labor market participation rates, and international competitiveness—in all these domains and more, the economies of northern and western Europe were incredibly successful.[12] And in spite of their slowdown in the very recent past, their performance is still comparable to that of the United States. The economic success of this form of capitalism is at least partly responsible for its survival over time. Had social democracy been an economic disaster, it would not have survived for long. But its basic institutions continue to enjoy massive support in the general population, despite the constriction of its redistributive mechanisms.

If social democracy had been a short-lived phenomenon, perhaps like the highly controlled wartime system in the United States that was quickly dismantled once the war ended or the Soviet-style command economies that lasted barely more than a half century, it would not pose a theoretical problem for a structural class theory.[13] Indeed, its short life span would be a vindication of the argument that capitalism selects for institutional varieties that are consistent with its basic logic. But the fact that its duration is approaching one hundred years in some parts of Europe, that it continues to be quite profitable for employers, and that its extinction does not seem imminent—even though its weakening is undeniable—poses a challenge. What does it mean to say that the class structure puts limits on institutional variation when the variation is so extensive as to include forms that seem to contradict some of the system's deepest tendencies?

One response would be to simply deny the premise that the range of variation is very significant. This strategy would rely on the fact that, whatever institutional variety we might see, however egalitarian social democracy might be, it is still short of "socialism." The basic idea would be that, in preventing social democracy from achieving the levels of economic redistribution we might reasonably desire, the constraints imposed by the class structure are, in fact, significant. This being the case, there is no real challenge to the theory since the theory only predicts that the class structure screens out institutions that undermine its basic logic. Since we know that social democracy was highly profitable, and hence did not threaten capitalist interests, and also see that its egalitarian thrust had real limits, we can safely assert that the theory stands confirmed in its fundamentals: social democracy had the support of the employer class, as any capitalism must, and it put limits on what labor could demand, as every capitalism does.

There is some merit to this response. It is true that social democracy screened out economic and political outcomes that would be highly desirable, would be more consistent with widely held conceptions of justice, and would most likely have substantial support within the population. But, while true, this argument cannot be enough to dismiss the theoretical challenge. It seems somewhat dogmatic to insist that as long as a redistributive regime is "still capitalism," the argument for the system's constraints stands vindicated. The whole point of the challenge is to explain how such remarkable levels of redistribution could be achieved at all in a system where the micrologic of the firm drives owners to engage in wage suppression. A critic might respond to the dismissal by insisting that if this is capitalism, why object to it? It is falling short of socialism, to be sure, but why use that as the contrast case? Why not compare it with the barbarity of free-market Victorian economies or all the depredations of an unregulated twenty-first-century capitalism? If social democracy looks like thin gruel compared to full-blown socialism, it looks like a wondrous advance compared to the free-market alternatives.

Further, a critic might go on to observe that the socialist counterfactual is, in any case, purely imaginary. While we are free to compare redistributive capitalisms with it, we do not, in fact, know that the more ambitious ideal of socialism is even *achievable*. We have not yet seen any examples of it. The Soviet-style economies did achieve a significant reduction in inequalities but also failed to lift the aggregate standards of living over time. What they gained in egalitarianism they lost in economic dynamism. And this gave the system a tendency to level living standards downward, rather than lifting them up. So—the critic would continue—far from a capitalism falling short of a more desirable end, what we witnessed in social democracy at its peak might, in fact, be approaching the best we can do. To focus on what it screens out is interesting but of no practical significance.

Hence, the mutability of capitalism does pose a challenge to structural class theory. We need to explain what is gained by insisting on the limits imposed by the class structure when the system is clearly so malleable.

4.5

Contingency within Limits

The answer is this: the constraining effects of the class structure are not only felt in how they screen out "socialist" possibilities; they are also critical in deciding how, and when, reforms are possible *within* capitalism. As presented in the first two chapters, a central consequence of the class structure is that, in distributing economic resources to social actors, it also distributes political capacity—it therefore determines the ability of class actors to pursue their interests and the conditions under which they can succeed. Which means that attempts to push the system in a more egalitarian direction, even when there is no intention of breaking out of capitalism, will confront a very specific set of conditions implanted by the class structure itself—most notably, a strong impulse from employers to resist any such attempts, and the need, on the part of labor, to rely on collective action to overcome that resistance. Furthermore, even when labor succeeds in installing a more equalitarian regime, its stability is very closely tied to labor's ability to shore it up. And in those situations where the political salience and organizational power of labor declines, we should expect the stability of social democratic regimes to suffer. The class structure therefore constrains institutional variation in two ways—by setting actors' interests with respect to any reforms and by forcing an unequal power relation between the contestants even when they pursue these more limited reforms. In so doing, it sets the conditions in which social democracy can be established and sustained. This is another way of saying that it explains not just what is screened *out* but also the range of variation *within* the system.

Class in the Rise of Social Democracy

The minimal claim in defense of a structural theory is that, if correct, it predicts that any significant shift in an egalitarian direction will elicit resistance from employers. This is because egalitarian redistribution tends to have two effects. First, it reduces workers' dependence on the labor market since they are granted access to basic goods as citizenship rights. Thus, in the most advanced social democracies, workers were able to acquire access to health care, housing, education, childcare, and other amenities as a right. They were assured access to these goods regardless of their employment status. This has the effect of indirectly increasing their bargaining power against their employers because workers' physical well-being was no longer fully dependent on having steady employment. They could take greater risks in making demands on their bosses since they were now less threatened by the prospect of being fired in retaliation.

A second motivation for employer resistance is that all social democracies tried—albeit in varying degrees—to reduce employers' unilateral authority over economic decisions. Two domains were crucial in this regard: decisions about wages and about investment. The means by which employers' power was reduced in these domains varied, as did the degree to which it was achieved. So, in some countries—the Nordic ones being exemplars, but also other western European ones and even the United States—wages had to be negotiated at the sectoral level, through peak bargaining between employer associations and unions. In others, it was more localized, but there were laws in place to extend the agreed-upon wages to the wider sectoral level—France being a prominent example. With regard to investment, once again, the mechanisms could be very different. In some cases, like France, investment autonomy was primarily constrained through national planning, to which privately owned firms had to adjust; in others, like West Germany, the constraint was primarily at the firm level through the installation of works councils—statutory bodies in which managers had to share some power with worker representatives over a host of firm-level economic decisions. But while the degree and the means could be different across cases, the principle remained the same—social democracy entailed a direct encroachment on managerial autonomy.

The theory thus predicts that employers will resist a turn toward social democracy; following from this, the installation of the institutions associated with it will depend upon the mobilization of a countervailing power from labor to overcome that resistance. What does the record show? Consistent with the theory, we find that, across the board, in most cases that have been studied, a shift in a social democratic direction required overcoming resistance from the employer class. And even more, the agency through which this was achieved was massive collective action—always by organizations of laboring classes and typically, though not always, in concertation with parties of the Left.[14] Of course, the Nordic countries are a prime example of this phenomenon, but the centrality of labor and Left parties is evident across the gamut of cases. The sole and partial exception is the United Sates, where, of course, no mass socialist party ever emerged to shepherd the institutionalization of social democracy. But the pivotal role of labor mobilization was perhaps even more salient in the United States, in large part *because* of the absence of a Left party within the state as an additional resource. Whereas, in other countries, socialist and communist parties could exercise their own leverage to push for egalitarian policies, in the United States, the labor movement had to gather up the power to induce an initially reluctant Democratic Party, under Franklin Roosevelt, to come to its side.[15]

The consistent opposition from capitalists, and the necessity of labor mobilization in the face of this recalcitrance, was a consequence of the class structure. Employers resisted egalitarian demands because of how the latter might affect their economic interests—interests generated by employers' structural location. This was an instance of the class structure *setting the terms* on which a social democratic turn might be effectuated. It ruled out other more consensual paths to the same outcome because it made it rational for one group of actors to oppose any move in that direction. It also ruled out, or at least rendered highly improbable, the possibility of the state pursuing an egalitarian path on its own initiative—again because the very same structure that motivated employers to oppose egalitarian policies also propelled them into a privileged position in the policy process. Precisely because of their greater wealth and their control over productive investment, employers in every capitalist economy were far better positioned than their employees to influence social policy. Hence, effectuating these demands at any significant scale required political leverage—which is why it was not until the modern labor movement got off the ground that the welfare state could emerge across the capitalist world.

In sum, the class structure generated a very specific alignment of interests, and the capacities to pursue them, in what was perhaps the central political development in the twentieth century—the rise of social democracy across capitalist nations. But while this goes some distance in establishing the causal—and hence also the explanatory—importance of structure, it does not, by itself, vindicate the underlying theory. It could be that while employer hostility was endemic on the road *toward* social democracy, that hostility might be substantially reduced, or even melt away, after some experience with it over time. Suppose employers found that their misgivings about egalitarian policies had been overdrawn—that, in fact, these policies did not undermine their basic interests and, indeed, sometimes were more successful in this regard than prior institutional arrangements. We might reasonably expect that employers would adjust their preferences in the wake of this discovery. They might very well end up supporting the egalitarian institutions and even try to sustain them if they began to weaken.

Such a change in employer preferences would have quite significant consequences for our theory. It would mean that the structurally generated conflict around egalitarian regimes was a temporary phenomenon caused by employers having imperfect information about its properties. Over time, as they discovered its virtuous properties, the social and political alignments that oversaw its installation would gradually dissolve. Employers who had opposed social democracy might now become quite supportive of it. Social democracy would therefore have two phases in its biography—a prehistory, as it were, in which concerted class struggle was required to anchor it in capitalism, and its maturation, during which old, class-based antagonisms dissolved. This is to say that *class* would cease to be a very binding constraint on future innovations within the system. Social democracy might still ebb and flow in its scope and ambitiousness, but its fortunes would not be driven by *class* conflict. Its evolution would be driven by other factors—sectoral alignments, with some firms on one side and some on the other; or purely political factors like party strength or voter coalitions; or demographic constraints like aging populations pressing against fiscal resources. Multiple configurations of the system might emerge—all mutations of modern social democratic capitalism but now unmoored from the conflicts and capacities generated by the older, antediluvian system. The many variations of the system would become genuinely contingent with respect to the class structure.

This counterfactual is not purely imaginary. As I observed earlier, social democracy turned out to be very successful on economic grounds. And it appeared to have at least tacit support from national capitalists in the sense that overt, concerted attempts to undermine it were not in evidence. If anything, it was the less egalitarian, less redistributive form of capitalism in the United States where capitalist hostility was most apparent. The American business community unleashed a coordinated campaign in the 1970s to roll back New Deal institutions and catapulted Ronald Reagan to the presidency to carry out the agenda. But in Europe, with the exception of Great Britain, the waters remained relatively tranquil. Even into the 1990s, Continental welfare states showed few signs of either breaking down or coming under attack in the same way as their American and British counterparts. This divergence led many scholars to wonder if capitalists had stumbled onto a novel, self-sustaining innovation—a kind of egalitarian, coordinated capitalism, as opposed to the inegalitarian, liberal capitalism of the United States.[16] And precisely because this newer form was also very efficient, there was no reason for employers to undermine it. It was a new variety of capitalism—egalitarian but also politically stable. In the next section, I examine the validity of these arguments.

Class in the Decline of Social Democracy

If history had stopped in the early 1990s, there would have been good reason to suppose that capitalism had indeed settled into two distinct and stable forms. And it might even have been reasonable to suggest that capitalists on the Continent had come to terms with their more egalitarian and regulated variant of it. But developments since that time have not been friendly to those propositions. Certainly by the early 2000s, the egalitarian thrust of the Continental political economies had not only weakened but was in many cases undergoing a reversal. And this was occurring on both dimensions of the concept—income differentials and power differentials between labor and capital. What is more, these changes took place under considerable pressure from the business community, and this is still true today. Far from having embraced their variety of capitalism, they seem to be working—much as their American counterparts did two decades earlier—to wrest free of its constraints and reestablish their supremacy.

It is important to be clear about what I am arguing. Certainly, if one made a static comparison between Continental social democracy and the American model today, we would find continuing differences on most every count. There has not been a convergence toward the same institutional form. But there is no mistaking that the *direction of change* has been noticeably away from the egalitarianism of the postwar decades toward a less redistributive system, with a shrinking space for labor in the political economy. The most extensive and persuasive analysis of the latter phenomenon is by Chris Howell and Lucio Bacarro. Taking up the changes in industrial relations over the past four decades or so, Howell and Bacarro found that in five key social democratic countries, labor unions have consistently lost ground to employers, regardless of the institutional setup.[17]

The essential precondition for the neoliberal turn has been a decline in the organizational strength of labor. As is widely recognized, union density, defined as the proportion of the labor force that has trade union membership, has been in steady decline in most advanced capitalist countries since the 1980s.[18] The United States started early along this path, followed by Great Britain and then the Continent. But what is equally important is the capitalist response to labor's waning power. It has been to either push in the same direction, so that unions lose even more traction in the political economy, or to move swiftly to take advantage of the changing power balance, thereby dismantling the wider social democratic institutions labor had put in place. Thus, recent scholarship has established that while employers on the Continent seemed to resist the urge to follow the Reagan-Thatcher program in the 1980s, and thereby appeared to have accepted social democracy, events took a very different turn in the 1990s and beyond. Across the social democratic countries, what seemed to be a case of employer support for the more redistributive capitalisms rapidly morphed into varying degrees of hostility.

The particular strategies chosen by elites were situationally specific. In Britain and France, the charge to dismantle social democratic institutions seems to have been taken by political parties, with employers waiting to see if the waters were safe and then diving in as labor's weakness became clear. The difference between the two was that, in Britain, it was led by the Conservative Party, while in France, it became a bipartisan endeavor very soon after the Mitterrand experiment crashed and burned.[19] But, in both, employers formed the critical support base of the turn to the right, and once it was underway, they became ever more ambitious in their goals. In Germany and Sweden, capitalists played a more active role in initiating the attack. Swedish employers seemed to have been spurred to action in the late 1970s as the Social Democrats unveiled the Meidner Plan, an initiative that proposed to gradually transfer control over capital to Swedish unions. After mobilizing successfully to block its adoption, employers gradually ramped up their political campaign. They led the charge to dismantle Sweden's famed corporatist institutions, the centerpiece of which was the sectoral peak bargaining system, and by the early 1990s had succeeded in the endeavor.[20] Germany followed a similar path of employer-led restructuring. Reunification with the East opened up a vast zone of nonunionized labor in the newly incorporated regions, which put downward pressure on wages, and employers lost no time in demanding concessions from workers in the very core of the manufacturing sector. Sectoral wage bargaining became unsustainable with the enormous disparity in wages between East and West, and employers were able to acquire considerable autonomy from national agreements. By the early 2000s, German unions were holding on as best they could but were unable to hold off employers' escalating attacks, not just on bargaining institutions but also on the welfare state itself.[21]

Now, there is ample ground for debate about the specifics of each case. But the basic fact of capitalists' participation in the dismantling of redistributive institutions is beyond dispute. This reaction from employers is important because it undermines the prediction that they might learn to accept social democracy once it is in place owing to its growth-enhancing effects. Had they learned to appreciate the latter, one might reasonably expect that, at least in a substantial plurality of the cases, their reaction to labor's weakened state would be to step in and shore up social democratic institutions. So, where labor's hand was failing, they would compensate for its reduced effectiveness. What we find, however, is a consistent pattern in their reactions—across the board, they showed an enduring hostility to the redistributive institutions. Wherever they thought they could make inroads into the foundations, without risking economic disruption from labor, they proceeded to do so. And this lends considerable support to the view that the class basis of social democracy never changed. Its fortunes have remained tied to the organizational strength of the labor movement. Employers participated in it as long as they had to, but they never embraced it.

Unsurprisingly, as labor's place in economic institutions has receded, income inequality has increased. In Sweden, long the bellwether of labor's egalitarian ambitions, Goran Therborn notes that inequality in 2013 had returned to levels not seen since the 1930s, the years of social democracy's inception.[22] More generally, Jonas Pontusson has found that "across OECD countries, levels of earnings inequality and redistribution are indeed associated with levels of unionization," as predicted by a class theory.[23] As unionization levels have declined, inequality has increased. In perhaps the most extensive study yet undertaken on this association, Evelyn Huber, Jingjing Huo, and John Stephens come to the same conclusion. In seeking to explain the skyrocketing incomes of the top 1 percent in OECD countries, they find that the most accurate predictor of its rise is the relative place of unions in the political economy:

> We find that the rise of the top 1% over the past half century has been driven by a decline in the relative power and resources of labor in the political economy in the form of declining union density and declining union and bargaining centralization and by prolonged incumbency of secular center and right parties.[24]

The two dimensions of egalitarianism—equalization of bargaining power and equalization of income—are thus tied together. The reduction in income and wealth inequality in the middle decades of the twentieth century, so famously demonstrated by Thomas Piketty, Emmanuel Saez, and others, was made possible by the antecedent increase in the bargaining power of labor. But as unions lost ground, and with it their power to affect income distribution, inequality returned to its pre–social democratic levels. Or, to return to the issue at hand, as labor's organizational power receded, the structural power of capital once again set the basic patterns of distribution.

All this occurred even while the institutional structure of European political economies remained distinct from that of the United States. One of the most important findings of Howell and Bacarro's research is that the revived power of employers is not expressed through any particular institutional mutation. Or, put differently, employers are dominating industrial relations *regardless* of the legal and institutional form—whether through works councils, sectoral bargaining, plant-level bargaining, state-regulated labor relations, or so forth.[25] Hence, it is a mistake to associate the persistence of institutional diversity with social democracy's durability. Many scholars have noted, correctly, that the institutional makeup of Continental capitalism has not converged to the American model. But Howell and Bacarro show that the recrudescence of employer dominance is proceeding despite this variability by simply overwhelming the particular form taken by industrial relations. This ability to overwhelm it is a direct consequence of the change in the balance of class power. Hence, there is plenty of variation in form but an increasing convergence in substance.

Hence, the class structure and the interests generated by it are critical to understanding both the rise and the decline of social democracy. This rounds out the argument of the section: that even while capitalism is compatible with a wide array of social institutions, its borders are not so capacious as to be irrelevant. Class actors are indifferent to many changes in culture and institutions, and changes confined to these groups will typically not elicit any systematic response from the former—and therefore will be contingent with respect to the class structure. But changes or variations that have an impact on the direct interests of class actors will tend to trigger a response and will therefore be more likely to be constrained by the class structure. Just how binding those constrains are will depend on the ability of the actors to pursue their interests—which, as we have seen, are not equally distributed. Hence, changes that impinge on the profit-making activities of capitalists will tend to face greater obstacles because capitalists are the best positioned actors to defend their priorities; changes that negatively affect labor will elicit a collective response only under certain conditions, and if those conditions are absent, they will trigger more individualized responses. This asymmetry in class capacities will translate into an asymmetry in the kinds of institutional changes we see and the sustainability of those changes.

The basic point is that contingency and agency are not in any way problematic for structural class analysis. Indeed, if my argument in this chapter is right, then a careful deployment of structural analysis is indispensable to the very project of recovering the scope and efficacy of social agency. The next chapter suggests how we might move in that direction.

5

How Capitalism Endures

Perhaps the most important legacy of classical Marxism is its insistence that conflict is built into the very heart of modern capitalism. The focus on conflict stems naturally from Marx's conception of class, in which the dominant group advances its interests at the expense of subordinate groups. The very act of defending their respective interests pits the main social classes against each other. Given the emphasis on conflict, it is not surprising that Marx and his followers also took the system to be inherently unstable. Over time, as it matured, so did the conditions for its supersession. Chief among these was the growth of the industrial proletariat, which not only had an interest in overthrowing the system but also the capacity to do so. And indeed, for the first half century or so after Marx's death, the emphasis on instability seemed to be amply borne out. From the 1890s to the 1930s, not only did the system seem to be teetering on collapse, but the very contours of social conflict appeared to amply vindicate Marx's expectations—it was the emerging industrial proletariat that was at the helm of the revolutionary outbreaks across the capitalist world.

For the early generations of class theorists, then, the lesson was obvious—the economic structure was the source of contradiction and instability. It followed that whatever the sources of system stabilization might be, they would be found *outside* the basic structure. And they would be swimming against a powerful tide in that they would have to neutralize the contradictions at the very core of the system itself. As I argued in Chapter 3, the postwar Left, for all its criticism of the early Marxists, accepted this basic premise more or less in toto. Thus, while they correctly insisted that classical Marxists had dramatically underestimated the system's ability to survive and then undertook to explain the latter phenomenon, they sought the answer in the "superstructure," not in the economic foundation of capitalism. This was a tacit *acceptance* of the classical framework even though it was fulsomely expressed as a repudiation of it.

I have argued in this book that the premise common to both traditions is mistaken. The real source of social order in capitalism—of its stable reproduction over time—is not culture or ideology, it is the class structure itself. The structure ensures that individuals within the working class choose individualized forms of resistance over collective ones. They do so not because they fail to recognize their interests, as theories of false consciousness or cultural hegemony would have it, but because they accurately perceive the risk / cost matrix associated with collective action. Hence, they typically opt for individualized forms of advancement over collective ones. But to opt for an individualized strategy is nothing other than to accept the dominant position of the employer—and of capitalists as a class. It leaves unchallenged the employer's structural power over the worker and seeks simply to maximize the worker's welfare within the latter's parameters. It is a tacit acceptance of the rules of the game, rather than an effort to transform or even challenge them.

It follows that class formation—of the kind predicted by early Marxists—is anything but automatic. It happens when workers become inclined to choose collective strategies over individual ones for the pursuit of their interests. But this requires a set of circumstances only contingently available and even now poorly understood. Broadly, collective action becomes more likely when the risks and costs associated with it are reduced, when workers feel a sense of confidence in their capacity, and when they develop a sense of common purpose and mutual commitment deep enough to make the sacrifices that are inevitable in any labor struggle. Now, some of the circumstances that reduce the material impediments and increase the sense of solidarity have, at certain times and in certain places, fallen into place without conscious effort by labor. Sometimes capitalism itself creates the conditions that increase the chances of class formation. But this cannot be taken for granted. More often, it takes conscious agency to bring them about. Whether they address the material disincentives or the psychological orientation, institutions undergirding class formation have to be built from the ground up and then sustained over time in the face of considerable resistance from a far more powerful agent—the employer class.

The fact that the institutions enabling working-class formation have to be built up and then sustained over time—the fact that they are not naturally occurring—means their construction is intrinsically problematic. They are hard to build, and the project of sustaining them as effective fighting organizations is even harder, which means they are highly vulnerable to destruction. Mistakes are therefore very costly—a badly timed strike can destroy a union, a corrupt leadership can demoralize the members, even the death of a leader can send an organization into decline. And the resulting losses can make the entire enterprise appear to be a Sisyphean undertaking. In sum, capitalism places the burden of class formation *entirely on the shoulders of the working class.* And this is why the process is highly contingent.

Employers, on the other hand, have less need to generate their own class organizations because their interests are preserved simply by the reproduction of the employment relation. The contrast with the conditions faced by labor is very stark. Capitalists do not have to organize themselves in order to advance their interests. Since the class structure places every employer in a position of dominance over his employees, collective action is unnecessary to secure an advantage over the latter. As long as workers show up to work every day, as long as they submit to the terms of the employment contract, they also serve to advance the capitalist's economic interests. This is the basic asymmetry between the two classes.

Precisely because of this structural asymmetry, how the classes utilize their political agency is also very different. For labor, any advance of their interests depends on building up and then sustaining institutions that enable collective action. The working class has to direct its political agency toward creating political organizations and then defending them. But, relative to labor, capital is relieved of this burden. Employers do benefit from creating class organizations of their own to coordinate their activities against labor. But this is not a precondition to their sustaining their position, much less advancing it. Their greater power is built into the class structure itself. Because this relieves them of the need to build organizations the way labor has to, they can direct their political agency toward *blocking and breaking up* the institutions labor is straining to create. Employers like Walmart, Amazon, Ford, Citibank, and even smaller entities can direct enormous resources toward preventing others' collective action instead of engineering their own.

This has a very important implication for the more mundane exigencies of political contestation. Because their power is located in the class structure itself, and not in political organization, employers are relieved of the burden of creating class organizations to advance their interests. The corollary to this is that, when they do create such organizations—parties, trade associations, lobbying groups, and so forth—they are less dependent on the quality and ability of these entities. Parties can fail, their leaders can turn out to be corrupt, even the president can have the mind and temperament of a child—but it does not typically pose a deep threat to the power and dominance of the class. As long as the class beneath them continues to show up for work and produce the revenues that sustain the system, it gives capitalists the time and space to fix the breakdowns—to replace incompetent managers, weather any scandals, build better parties, and so forth.

The advantages for employers stand in stark contrast to the conditions faced by labor. Advancing the interests of labor is entirely dependent on collective action, making the quality and ability of *their* organizations essential. Whereas the dominant class can weather organizational breakdown and political errors, the labor movement has no such luxury. A strategic error can lead to political defeat, and defeat can lead to demoralization and a reluctance to take risky actions the next time; organizations can suffer decline and breakdown—meaning that the work of rebuilding them, with all its risks and costs, has to be undertaken anew. Institutions that take decades to build up can be destroyed in a matter of weeks through repression, harassment, scandals, corruption, or any number of causes. But unlike capitalists, who have the class structure to fall back on, labor faces a yawning abyss underneath its class organizations.

Even when labor overcomes the political resistance of employers and cobbles together its class organizations, they are eroded by other properties of the class structure. Chief among these is technical change. Capitalists fight the competitive battle in product markets by upgrading technology, bringing in new machinery, and reorganizing production around them. The new technology has a dual effect—it phases out some occupations and the skills attached to them while generating demand for new ones. This process plays out at a micro level, but as it scales upward, it transforms the occupational structure itself. Skills become obsolete, particular occupations once in demand start to drop off, regions that were once economic hubs begin to stagnate, and economic backwaters become new centers of accumulation.

This process, unleashed by technical change, is built into the class structure; it is a direct and unavoidable result of capitalists' profit-maximizing drive. For labor, it creates an enormous political challenge. As the occupational structure changes, so does the constellation of interests attached to it. Alliances based on a certain spread of interests begin to fray, and new ones emerging and gaining traction create an entirely new terrain for organizers. Organizing strategies have to adjust around the new skills and new work conditions, new alliances have to be forged across the occupational groupings, and the cultural work that cements the class project has to take on entirely new challenges. The labor movement has to adjust continually to the dynamic properties of the class structure, and a failure to do so is to preside over its own diminution. Meanwhile, employers face no corresponding imperative, since their power is not founded on the success of their class cohesion but on the simple reproduction of the class relation itself.

This is how the capitalist class structure underwrites its own stability. The structures are constantly working *against* labor while largely *shoring up* the political power of capitalists. The class structure slants the political terrain systematically against the working class so that it has to bear the entire burden of creating and sustaining its political institutions, and it does so against a foe that is structurally and institutionally advantaged. Not surprisingly, the response from the modal worker is typically to choose prudence over valor—to prioritize holding on to what they have rather than risking it on the arduous work of collective action. This is not, in any way, a false consciousness—it is a sober appreciation of the terrain as it actually presents itself.

Hence, Marx was certainly right to insist that conflict is built into the class relation itself. But the conflict is everywhere and always lopsided. Or, to be more precise, capitalism endures because the same class structure that generates conflict *also distributes political capacities unequally* between the contending classes. The system locks the classes into an antagonistic relationship, but the unequal distribution of capacities ensures that the conflict, where it occurs, tends to be resolved in the employers' favor. The laboring class, for its part, has to bear the onus of figuring out how to organize itself—in an ever-shifting occupational structure and an evolving political terrain—against a political rival that has the structural forces set up in its favor.

Thus, one can commit to a materialist class theory and also affirm that there is no teleology, no set of deterministic forces pushing toward class formation. When and where the latter does occur, it comes from a set of conjunctural factors that enable labor to overcome the forces that typically inhibit organizational success. And as these circumstances change, as the enabling conditions weaken or are eroded by the constantly evolving character of the structure, the organizations that were built up around one set of circumstances become unstable. They have to either adjust to the new environment or face extinction.

In the early twentieth century, labor was able to figure out how to take advantage of the structural and institutional facts of the time and build organizations that brought workers together as a class. They were able to shoulder the burden of class formation. But as those conditions changed, the class institutions the Left had built up began to disintegrate, and the class itself changed in composition, so that the sectors where it was growing the fastest were those that fell outside the protection of its organizational apparatus. Today, when much of that apparatus is either significantly weakened or dismantled, the challenge is to build it anew, in dramatically changed conditions, and devise a strategy capable of navigating the current economic landscape.

With this theory in hand, we can present a consistently materialist account of the phenomena the postwar Left sought to answer through the prism of culture.

5.1

The Growth Phase of the First Left

Two points ought to be kept in mind for what is to follow. First, it is not meant to be a fully fleshed out argument but a rough framework for understanding the process of class formation and fragmentation over the course of a century. Second, the empirical phenomena it points to should be understood as "stylized facts"—basic trends and social developments that were differentially spread and temporally asynchronous but operative across the regions that are my focus.

I have argued that it was the very success of class organizing in the early twentieth century that led the classical Marxists to underestimate the stabilizing properties of capitalism. What accounts for this success? The circumstances and class environment that the trade unionists and socialists encountered in the early 1900s was significantly different from today. This combination of structural and institutional facts enhanced the process of class formation.

Heading the list were some key facts about the class structure it-self. In the parts of western Europe that served as the leading edge of the working-class movement, the economies were experiencing a profound transition from agriculture to urban manufacturing. These were rapidly industrializing countries. This meant, first and foremost, that the sectors of the economy that were expanding fastest were the most hospitable to class organizing. This is true, of course, when you compare manufacturing to agriculture. As Marx and countless social scientists since him have observed, industrial employment is far more conducive to unionization than agricultural labor. And since workers were primarily being drawn from agriculture into urban industry, they were transitioning from a low-density organizational environment to a high-density one. Further, the establishments where they worked solved some collective action problems for them. This was the era of massive factories that employed thousands of workers. For organizers, this provided important economies of scale—a small number of unionists could reach hundreds and thousands of workers in a small setting. And, finally, the fact that industrial employment was expanding rapidly meant the fear of long-term unemployment was mitigated to an appreciable extent. Getting fired for political activity was less of a deterrent to organizers than it would have been in a slow-growing or stagnant industrial sector. If they were sacked, they were confident that employment would be available elsewhere—probably in the same industrial district, where they could resume their organizing activities.

Layered on top of this structural fact about the capitalism of the time were some institutional facts. The most important was the po-litical status of the working class. Until the second decade of the century, workers in virtually the entire capitalist world were disen-franchised. This was true even in the United States, where white working men technically had the right to vote but effectively were pushed out of the system for two decades after 1896.[1] The *political* exclusion of the working class reinforced the sense of *economic* injustice emanating from the work conditions of the time. Both factors pushed in the same direction. Both instilled a sense within the class that the system was entirely captured by the propertied classes, for the same people who dominated them in the workplace also passed the laws within the state. This was a crucial factor in solidifying a sense of class identity among the poor.

Additionally, as many urban historians have pointed out, the residential layout of urban centers deepened the separation between the classes. There were many kinds of segregation in the growing urban centers at the turn of the twentieth century. Some facilitated working-class formation, and others undercut it. But the basic fact of class segregation is undeniable, and it extended well into the early decades of the century. Equally well established is the fact that, all else being equal, the rise of working-class ghettos and slums contributed mightily to the growing sense of common condition and interests among its inhabitants. It was not just the experience of common economic condition and social isolation; it was also the ubiquitous growth of the self-help and mutual aid societies workers had to develop, all of which centered around home and neighborhood and tied them materially to one another in everyday life.[2]

These factors had two properties in common that interest us here: first, they were absolutely central facts about working-class life in the decades straddling the turn of the century, and second, *they all pushed in the same direction*—they conspired to generate a sense of common status and common condition, and hence a common identity, within the working class. This made it a great deal easier to organize individuals in the same structural situation into a class. Many dimensions of their economic and social life reinforced the sense that they were suffering the same liabilities and injustices and shone a light on the groups that held power over them. This power was revealed as concentrated and manifold in that it radiated into every aspect of their social condition.

These overlapping and reinforcing institutional factors comprised the bedrock on which trade unionists built early twentieth-century class organizations. Whether working-class parties or trade unions, these nascent vehicles for class mobilizations drew on the raw material provided by the workers' common condition. But it is important to note that the actual work of *organizing them* was indispensable to the outcome. Whatever the structural conditions, however cloistered the social life, however deep the sense of political marginalization— these factors could not and still do not *of themselves* create class formation. The baseline obstacles to that outcome remain very much in place: the crushing imbalance of power at work, the insecurity on which it is based, the background of asset scarcity that makes even a short bout of unemployment so costly, and so on. All these factors make it alluring to opt for an individualized resistance strategy rather than a collective one, even in the conditions of the early 1900s.

The actual success in class formation, therefore, was very much an achievement. Had it not been for the concerted efforts of the organizers at the time, the enabling conditions might have remained politically inert. One of the signal developments of that era was the simultaneous birth of mass working-class parties and the trade union movement. Each fed and reinforced the other. While neither of the two institutions had much of a purchase in the political economy around the turn of the century, they had become mass phenomena by the 1930s. Together, they not only created the most effective political vehicle that labor has ever seen in the modern era but, alongside that, sustained the very culture of solidarity and mutualism that is essential for effective collective action. Almost all the labor movement's mass organizations today were born in those decades, and the movement has never managed to build anything even approaching them in terms of their scale, scope, depth, and ambition. This was the final, indispensable element that contributed to class formation in the early part of the century.

The political outcome of this enormous growth in working-class organization was, for the first time in modern history, a significant redistribution of income and wealth toward the lower rungs of society. The nascent labor organizations leveraged their newfound power into rewriting not just the labor contract but the social contract more broadly. Material gains in the workplace were complemented by a qualitative leap in access to basic services outside it—in housing, health care, transportation, and so on. The latter gains were now institutionalized as rights and became embedded into the very idea of citizenship.[3] Together, this institutional ensemble comprised the foundation of social democracy, which so dramatically changed the contours of capitalism that, by the end of the twentieth century, many social scientists considered it a new social form altogether.[4]

Social democracy was sustained as a kind of political exchange between capital and labor—a negotiated compromise in which employers were forced to accommodate labor's interests in exchange for labor agreeing to industrial peace. As I argued in Chapter 3, if ever there was an instance of cultural hegemony in capitalism—an era in which the system relied on the active consent of labor—the four decades after World War II comes closest to it. Workers witnessed the greatest advance in their standards of living that they had ever seen, which served to boost capitalism's legitimacy to an extent that would have been unimaginable during the century's first decades.

The important point is that this consent, to the extent that it was real, was dependent upon a set of very material factors. It was a hegemony *expressed* in the culture, but it was not the *product* of culture. Its conditions of existence were organizational and economic. Organizationally, it was the trade union movement and its accoutrements—the various labor parties being the most important. Economically, it was the unprecedented growth of the postwar decades, which expanded national income at a pace rapid enough to fund the rapidly expanding welfare state while also expanding corporate profits.

As long as the economic pie kept expanding, the competing demands of labor and capital could both be sustained—they did not turn into a zero-sum game. But starting in the late 1960s, this began to change. With the manufacturing sector as its epicenter, a slowdown in economic growth slowly enveloped the advanced economies. Corporate profits, hitherto generous and bountiful, began to contract noticeably; starting in the United States, and then slowly fanning out into the rest of the West, employers began to experience a squeeze on their profit margins, which triggered a dramatic reversal in their attitude to the political exchange with labor.[5] Whereas union demands on them had been obnoxious but tolerable during the 1950s, they now became intolerable as profits margins shrank. Employers who felt hesitant to upset the apple cart in earlier years now felt they were willing to risk a confrontation with unions—and the possibility of its triggering economic disruption.

US employers thus led the charge against the postwar class settlement, with Margaret Thatcher's Britain in train. Using aggressive tactics at the workplace and every lever that labor law provided them, they beat back the union presence in their establishments. And, indeed, while there was a muted retaliation by the labor movement, the actual economic disruption turned out to be minimal. By the mid-1980s, union membership in the United States had declined precipitously, almost down to pre–New Deal levels. Continental Europe followed a decade later. By the turn of the millennium, organized labor had shrunk to a fraction of its size across much of the advanced industrial world—even in the Nordic countries, hitherto the bastion of trade union prowess.

5.2

From Consent to Resignation

As the organizational strength of the working class waned, the normative foundation for capitalist reproduction also underwent a change in emphasis. The role of "consent" shrank because the basis for an ongoing political exchange between labor and capital was now dramatically weakened. It was replaced, increasingly, by employers' diktat. The proportion of the working population represented and protected by labor unions shrank in size, leaving employees to negotiate their labor contracts as individuals. This could only mean a dramatic weakening of their bargaining power relative to their employer and, for the latter, a renewed power to offer "take it or leave it" terms of employment. Therefore, consent was displaced by resignation—since "leave it" is simply not an option for the typical wage laborer, they had to "take" what they were offered.

And what they were offered was a return to the status quo ante and the conditions typical of the era before unions. In the United States, which led the charge to restore the ancient regime, the postwar gains in wages and general employment came to a virtual halt in the mid-1970s, along with a deterioration in several other indices of economic welfare. The retreat in income was jarring enough, but it was more than matched by what was happening to wealth. As recent research has established, the share of wealth captured by the top one-tenth of 1 percent (.1 percent) of the population in 2010 had reached the same levels as just before the Great Depression—a retreat to the state of affairs almost a century ago, erasing the gains made in the decades since.[6] By 2010, white working-class males actually experienced a decline in average life expectancy—something not witnessed in this section of the population in more than a hundred years.[7]

The labor force absorbed all this. They took the wage stagnation and explosion in wealth inequality, the decline in work conditions, and everything that accompanied it. They continued to soldier through it even when labor markets tightened. Not only was there no countermovement from labor unions—or the working class more broadly—to the employer offensive, but the incidence of industrial disruption continued its decline to historic lows. Workers seemed to have appreciated Margaret Thatcher's TINA dictum[8]—they understood that having a job, however miserable, was better than no job at all.[9] In a climate of generalized insecurity and atomization, they were unwilling to hazard their employer's disapproval, even when a tight labor market reduced the risk. This was a labor exchange stripped down to Marx's "dull compulsion of economic relations."

But any system whose normative foundation is resignation, rather than consent, faces certain limits. For years, the working population accepted the deal they were given because they did not see an option. On the surface, this took on the appearance of consent—or, at least, of satisfaction. But what was, in fact, happening was a slow and quite deep erosion of support for mainstream institutions. Academic specialists had some inkling of this, as opinion polls showed a steady decline in the relevant indicators.[10] But there was no political explosion, no mass upheaval or Polanyian "Second Movement" in reaction to steadily worsening conditions. The more common response was, instead, to turn inward—to give up on political participation and civic association, to hunker down and try to hold on as best as possible. It showed up in declining voter turnout across the capitalist world, erosion of party identification, a withering of civic institutions—the "bowling alone" phenomenon—and sundry other manifestations of ennui and cynicism. But because it was a slow accretion of discontent, expressed individually and aggregated only as a statistical phenomenon, it could go unnoticed and hence was ignored.

Only in the very recent past, perhaps since the 2011 Occupy Wall Street movement, has there been a significant public manifestation of dissatisfaction with the status quo. But the speed with which it has overtaken political culture is quite dramatic. Across the advanced industrial world, large swathes of the public, especially among the working class, have rejected the mainstream political and economic institutions. This is, of course, a continuation of the trend that was set during the neoliberal era. But the form has changed from passive to active—from opting out of public engagement to varied and uneven support for new political agencies. In the main, this has been an electoral defection, wherein the rapidly hollowing center is giving way to political forces that had been either marginal or nonexistent until recently. So declining support for the status quo has lifted the fortunes of electoral rivals that had once seemed confined to the wilderness.

On balance, the turn of events thus far has mostly benefited the Far Right. Since the 1990s, as the political mainstream has lost working-class support, that support has dramatically moved to an emergent cluster of parties and organizations wedded to xenophobic and racist political platforms. But alongside that, building in momentum, there has also been, for the first time in several decades, a noticeable uptick in strike activity in the United States and, to a lesser extent, in Europe.[11] And even while teachers' strikes in several states received the most press, over the decade as a whole, private sector stoppages led the charge by a considerable margin over the public sector.[12] By historical standards, strike activity is still miniscule. It does not even match the levels of the 1980s, when the labor movement was in full retreat. But it is the first sign of its revival in almost four decades. Further, it is buoyed by an unmistakable cultural shift, in which a general social mobilization, both within organized politics and without, is occurring against the massive and growing inequities between the rich and the poor.

This is an unmistakable sign that the sense of helplessness within the laboring population is waning. The widely felt outrage, the mainstream's loss of legitimacy, the uptick in strike activity—all this portends perhaps a reversal of the trends of the past half century. It is tempting to wonder if the momentum of recent events could ignite a process of class formation, perhaps reminiscent of the era a century ago. The idea is no doubt premature, for the scale of organizing involved would be so massive that the actual bursts of activity witnessed thus far seem minuscule, even trivial. But what makes this episode feel different than anything we have seen in the recent past is two facts: it is multidimensional in scope, covering economic, cultural, and political aspects and not just confined to one of them; second, it is international in scale, with the mobilizations against neoliberal economic models having gained traction in virtually every continent and most of the industrial world. While it is certainly too early to announce a new wave of working-class formation, it would be folly to miss that this is a global turn against the neoliberal model.

It is tempting to wonder if these events might signify the onset of a new wave of working-class formation, either revitalizing institutions now in desuetude or crafting new ones as they did a century ago. It is certainly possible. It is clear that we are entering a period of significant political fluidity. But it is important to register that, even if the impulse to reassemble the labor movement intensifies, the terrain on which it will unfold has shifted significantly from the 1900s. This is best appreciated if we examine the current disposition of the very factors that facilitated class formation in that earlier period.

5.3
The Class Matrix Today

I suggested in Section 5.2 that three sorts of factors came together to facilitate the creation of labor institutions in the early twentieth century—structural, institutional, and organizational. It is reasonable to suppose that any effort to resuscitate labor could try to rely on those same factors, having on hand the template for success. The deep structural facts about capitalism, which generate the antagonism between labor and capital and motivate wage laborers to organize themselves, remain in place. But the way these structural features combine and the form in which they are reproduced have changed in some significant ways. On top of that, the more contingent institutional and organizational environment has mutated even more profoundly, making for a political environment that would scarcely be recognizable to the organizers who first built labor institutions.

To begin, there has been a profound shift in the occupational structure—from one that was *industrializing* in the 1920s to one that is *deindustrializing* in the 2020s. The advanced capitalist world began to shift away from industry toward services by the 1960s, and the pace of that transition was quite rapid by the century's end. This broad transformation of the occupational structure was accompanied by a slowdown in the pace of growth as well—so that the turn toward services went hand in hand with a slowdown in employment growth. Finally, the slower-growing, deindustrializing capitalism also shifted to smaller and more decentralized establishments, as opposed to the classic large manufacturing plants of the interwar years. What is even more interesting is that the shift toward services has also taken root in the Global South—a phenomenon that economists have dubbed "early deindustrialization."[13] It is described as being *early* in that the phenomenon occurred in the core economies after they had more or less fully transitioned out of agriculture, but in the South, the transition is taking place while a significant proportion of the labor force is still in rural activities—meaning that these countries will likely never have the weight of manufacturing employment of their predecessors in the West. Instead of industry sucking peasants out of agriculture into stable urban employment, the latter is already shedding labor en masse, swelling the ranks of the semi-employed or those in ramshackle informal jobs that barely provide a living wage.

These structural facts about today's capitalism make for a very different environment for class formation than the one confronting the trade unions a century ago. A slow-growth, small- workplace, service-based economy provides entirely new challenges than did the older classically manufacturing one, for obvious reasons. The economies of scale that large venues afforded to organizers are now harder to secure; instead of reaching thousands of employees at one go, they must now bring them together a few dozen or a few hundred at a time, one establishment at a time. Further, the reliance on outsourcing has meant that the venues are smaller and the officers managing the firms have little control over investment and workplace decisions, which often remain under the control of firms higher up in the value chain, against whom organizers may not have any direct leverage. In many cases, it is not even clear to whom the organizers can direct their demands.[14] Finally, downsizing and slower growth have led to much less job security—what is commonly called "precariousness"—which has revived the fear typical of Victorian-era employment, in which workers are far more cautious about making any demands on their employers.

These conditions are now very widespread in the advanced world. But the fact of early deindustrialization in the South means they are also truly global in scope. What makes this especially important is that it undermines any hope that the decline of propitious conditions for class formation in the advanced world might be balanced out by their shift into the developing countries. One might have supposed that, as the class structure transitions out of industry in the core economies, rapid industrialization in the Global South might, if nothing else, shift the locus of class formation to the South—thus sustaining an impulse for labor's reemergence in the global economy, even if displaced into new zones.

The changes are not confined to the class structure. Added to them are some very significant institutional changes compared to a century ago. If we confine ourselves to the two that I described as conducive to class formation in the earlier period, it is evident that they no longer perform the same function. At the turn of the previous century, the working class was still politically excluded on top of being economically exploited, and the former reinforced the sense of injustice generated by the latter. But by mid-century, workers across the developed world were fully vested citizens. The greater scope for inclusion in the political system was very ably utilized by them in pursuit of their interests—but they did so through organizations built up during the earlier era of political disenfranchisement. The challenge today is to build similar organizations once again but in a context where the sense of political exclusion is not perceived to anywhere near the same extent. To be sure, significant numbers of working adults have disengaged from the system due to a sense of futility in the face of elite dominance, but opting out is not the same as facing a legal bar. Whereas the latter fueled a sense of outrage and common purpose, the former tends to be more a sign of despair and, hence, individualistic.

So, too, with another institutional fact that fueled class identification—the residential patterns of urban centers. I argued that the physical layout of large industrial centers pushed workers together into crowded spaces while separating them from their employers. But by the 1960s, this was no longer the case. In a landmark 1987 essay, Eric Hobsbawm articulated what has become a sort of common sense among labor historians: that the flight of industry from urban centers, followed by the migration of securely employed working-class families to the suburbs, had a profound effect on class identities. Whereas, in earlier decades, the residential clusters and tenements surrounding the giant manufacturing hubs had tended to reinforce the sense of common status forged at work, this was no longer the case by mid-century. As employment itself became dispersed and housing radiated outward and beyond city boundaries, work life and social life became ever further separated. As Hobsbawm noted, "Urban development, public and private, was destroying the very bases which had allowed the formation of [the] 'urban villages' on which so much of labour strength had rested. . . . The effect of all this on labour movements in the great city [was] to deprive them of their former cohesion."[15]

If we consider these two factors together, the contrast with conditions a hundred years ago is stark. Workers' electoral status and social conditions once worked in tandem with the class structure to push workers toward a common identity, but this is no longer the case; now, the same dimensions of working-class life have the opposite effect—they reinforce the *atomizing* aspects of the class structure, pulling workers apart instead of pushing them together and, hence, deepening the inclination toward individualistic resistance. Whereas the social and political conditions then partially *solved* workers' collective action problems, today they tend to strengthen the *constraints*.

The point here is not that the obstacles to class formation have become insuperable. It is rather that the ground under labor's feet has shifted in new and unforeseen ways. Conditions that enabled organizing techniques to function in the past do not work today, or if they do, it is alongside quite novel developments that pose new challenges. Therefore, strategies of organizing that were effective in the past cannot be assumed to work today. While the events of the past few years provide ample evidence for working-class disaffection from the status quo and a corresponding motivation to seek new avenues for representation in the political economy, translating this motivation into collective action will require tactical innovation.

Once again, the burden of class formation falls squarely and asymmetrically on the shoulders of labor. They cannot simply return to the old script, but there is also no new script ready and available. Writing it, composing its architecture and form, falls entirely on them. And it does so asymmetrically because the employer class has no corresponding burden on its shoulders. There is no need for them to forge organizations to defend or advance their class interests because the class *structure* continues to do it for them. As long as their employees continue to show up for work every day, as long as the profitability of their enterprises is sustained—as long as the basic elements of the system grind along on a daily basis—their basic material interests are advanced correspondingly. It does not require political organizing. Their energies, therefore, can be directed at simply breaking up the organizing efforts of their employees, thus piling more layers of constraints on the ones spontaneously thrown up by the class structure itself.

So far, labor has not been able to solve the puzzle of class organizing in this new setting. The best its organizations have been able to do is to tread water or slow down the rate of decline. To the extent that members of the class have expressed their discontent, they have done so with the means available to them, and the only such means universally available at present is the ballot box. No wonder, then, that the discontent has tended to be electoral in form and that the explosion has been *populist* in content, whether on the left or right. The new populist wave of the past decade is the new face of working-class rebellion today. Whether it evolves into something more substantial will depend on labor's ability to solve the puzzle of class organizing in the new setting.

What makes it especially challenging in the current conditions is that the political vehicles committed to solving the organizational puzzle in the previous era are also missing today—the parties, syndicates, radical unions, mass organizations of the Left, and so forth that were the catalyst behind class formation. Insofar as labor organization was a political achievement, and not a necessary product of structural conditions, it was to be credited to the layers of dedicated organizers embedded in the communities and workplaces of the capitalist world. Today, insofar as there is a left in the core economies of the advanced industrial world, it is largely divorced from the working class. It is housed mainly in professional settings like university campuses and nonprofit organizations, not in the neighborhoods and productive establishments where labor confronts capital. Even electorally, as Thomas Piketty has very persuasively shown, the social democratic parties in the West no longer look to the working class as their base and are far more reliant on the professional, college-educated strata.[16] Hence, whereas there was once a natural and organic relationship between the self-styled "Left" and the working class, this is no longer the case.

There is undoubtedly a degree of endogeneity in this relationship. In other words, the very change in structural conditions is at least partially responsible for the absence of a labor Left of the kind that grew so rapidly a century ago. The fine-grained causal links are not well understood. But it seems plausible to imagine that the culture of resistance fostered by the structural and institutional setting in the early twentieth century also fostered the political organizations that gave it shape and direction. In part, it was by creating the conditions for a coalescence of worker-militants in the neighborhoods, workplaces, and clubs of the growing urban manufacturing centers. But it also attracted members of the middle class—radicals, students, and intellectuals—who were inspired by the ideals expressed by the growing labor organizations and provided a link that connected the working class to progressive sections of the intermediate economic strata. If this is so, it is quite likely that as the structural conditions changed and workers opted for more individualized forms of resistance, it also diluted the elements that had combined to produce the earlier layer of militants and labor organizers. And as the density of labor organizers was reduced, so the traditional vehicle for collective action become increasingly scarce—thereby reinforcing the spontaneous tendency to play it safe and resist individually.

Thus, the class matrix today constrains and shapes the political terrain much as it did a century ago—but in ways that differ substantially from that earlier period. Across much of the intellectual world, there is a growing consensus that the decline of labor organizations is one of the key factors behind the obscene concentration of wealth and income on one side and stagnant standards of living among the vast majority. So, too, there is a recognition that if there is to be a recovery of anything like the improvements witnessed in the postwar era, a revival of working-class institutions will play an indispensable role in it. It is on the question of how those institutions might be revived that we find a great deal of puzzlement. There is no reason to assume the strategies and organizational vehicles that were effective a century ago can simply be revived and redeployed in the world that labor currently inhabits.

Whatever the new strategies and institutions, they will only be discovered by closely examining the actual constraints that labor faces and then mapping out a sustainable path to navigating them. That is just the first step. Then comes the arduous task of attracting the multitudes of laboring families to the agenda, harnessing their energies to it, and sustaining the organizations over time as they advocate for their interests. One small but essential step toward this is to revive and deepen the tradition of political economic analysis that earlier partisans of labor took for granted—the conviction that capitalism is a system resting on a class structure; that the structure imposes real constraints on social actors; that those constraints are facts of life, not symbolic constructions; and that political contestation is fundamentally about harnessing political interests to political objectives. If that tradition of analysis is indeed essential to reviving progressive movements, social theory will have to find a way back from the excesses of the cultural turn.

Notes

Acknowledgments

Index

Notes

Introduction

1. Pierre Bourdieu, "The Social Space and the Genesis of Groups," *Theory and Society* 14 (1985): 723–744.

2. E. P. Thompson, *The Making of the English Working Class* (New York: Pantheon, 1964).

3. Thompson, *The Making*, 12.

4. Patrick Joyce, *Visions of the People* (Cambridge: Cambridge University Press, 1994), 16.

5. Joyce, *Visions of the People*, 16.

6. Clifford Geertz, "Deep Play: Notes on a Javanese Cockfight," in *The Interpretation of Cultures*, 3rd ed. (New York: Basic Books, 2000), 435–474.

7. For 1960, see Alain DeJanvry, Elizabeth Sadoulet, and Linda Wilcox Young, "Land and Labour in Latin American Agriculture from the 1950s to the 1980s," *The Journal of Peasant Studies* 16, no. 3 (Fall 1989): 396–424, Table 1. For the trends since 1990, see the World Bank Dataset on Employment in Agriculture in Latin American and the Caribbean, "Employment in Agriculture (% of Total Employment) (Modeled ILO Estimate)—Latin America & Caribbean," The World Bank, last modified January 29, 2021, https://data.worldbank.org/indicator/SL .AGR.EMPL.ZS?locations=ZJ. The data are not entirely consistent since collection and criteria have changed over time, but the broad direction of change is not in dispute.

8. See, inter alia, Tali Kristal, "Good Times, Bad Times: Postwar Labor's Share of National Income in Capitalist Democracies," *American Sociological Review* 75, no. 5 (October 2010): 729–763; Loukas Karabarbounis and Brent Neiman, "The Global Decline in the Labor Share," *Quarterly Journal of Economics* 1 (February 2014): 61–103.

9. William Sewell, *The Logics of History: Social History and social Transformation* (Chicago: University of Chicago Press, 2005), 49.

10. Sewell, *The Logics of History*, 49.

11. As evidenced in Nancy Fraser beginning a recent article with the declaration, "Capitalism is back!"; see her "Behind Marx's Hidden Abode; for an Expanded Definition of Capitalism," *New Left Review* 86 (March–April 2014): 55–72; or Richard Swedberg resorting to a sports metaphor, "A Comeback for Capitalism," *Contemporary Sociology* 41, no. 5 (September 2012): 609–613; or Jurgen Kocka and Marcel van der Linden (ed.), with their anodyne *Capitalism: The Re-emergence of a Historical Concept* (London: Bloomsbury, 2016).

1. Class Structure

1. William Sewell, "The Political Unconscious of Social and Cultural History, or, Confessions of a Former Quantitative Historian," in *The Logics of History* (Chicago: University of Chicago Press, 2005), 42. Emphasis added.

2. Patrick Joyce, *Visions of the People* (Oxford: Oxford University Press, 1994), 6.

3. This is a different formulation than the one I proposed in "Rescuing Class from the Cultural Turn," *Catalyst* 1, no. 1 (2017): 36, where I described the wage laborer's situation as one of structural *coercion*. It seems to me that his condition is better captured as compulsion rather than coercion. The latter should be reserved for relations of authority between social agents and not as the pressure exerted by circumstances.

4. I call this a particular reading of Weber because even while it offers a plausible interpretation of *The Protestant Ethic*, he is, in fact, somewhat inconsistent in arguing for the determining role of culture. But this will have to be taken up elsewhere.

5. For arguments that the cultural orientation of Hindus would be an obstacle to capitalistic development, see K. W. Kapp, *Hindu Culture, Economic Development and*

Economic Planning in India (Bombay: Asia Publishing House, 1963), and V. Mishra, *Hinduism and Economic Growth* (Bombay: Oxford University Press, 1962); for a less pessimistic view, albeit from someone who accepts that capitalism requires the prior existence of an appropriate cultural outlook, see Milton Singer, "Cultural Values in India's Economic Development," *Annals of the American Academy of Political and Social Science* 305 (May 1956): 81–91.

6. For a description of the causal logic of mediating mechanisms, see Erik Olin Wright, *Class, Crisis and the State* (London: Verso, 1978), 23–25.

7. I am grateful to Daniel Cheng for this suggestion.

8. I am grateful to Roberto Veneziani for pressing me to be more careful in my formulations here.

9. E. P. Thompson, *The Poverty of Theory* (London: Merlin Press, 1978), 130.

2. Class Formation

1. This criticism is so widespread that it has become something of a common idea in the field. But for cogent and influential arguments from two ends of the world, see Margaret Somers, "Narrativity, Narrative Identity, and Social Action: Rethinking English Working-Class Formation," *Social Science History* 16, no. 4 (Winter 1992): 591–630, esp. 594–598; and Dipesh Chakrabarty, *Rethinking Working-Class History* (Princeton, NJ: Princeton University Press, 1989), 220–222.

2. Adam Smith, *The Wealth of Nations* (Chicago, University of Chicago Press, 1977), vol. 1, chap. 8, 98–99.

3. For a good overview of the dynamics of incomplete contracts, see Joyce Jacobsen and Gilbert Skillman, *Labor Markets and Employment Relationships: A Comprehensive Approach* (Oxford: Basil Blackwell, 2004), 221–243.

4. The classic analysis is in Harry Braverman, *Labor and Monopoly Capital: The Degradation of Work in the Twentieth Century* (New York: Monthly Review Press, 1974)

5. For the health impact of job insecurity, see Jagdish Khubchandani and James H. Price, "Association of Job Insecurity with Health Risk Factors and Poorer Health in American Workers," *Journal of Community Health* 42 (2017): 242–251, and Sarah Burgard, Jennie Brand, and James House, "Perceived Job Insecurity and Worker Health in the United States," *Social Science and Medicine* 69, no. 5 (September 2009): 777–785. For a comparison of the relative harm from insecurity compared

to unemployment, see Tae Jun Kim and Olaf von dem Knesebeck, "Is an Insecure Job Better for Health Than Having No Job at All? A Systematic Review of Studies Investigating the Health-Related Risks of Both Job Insecurity and Unemployment," *BMC Public Health* 15 (2015): 985.

6. See my argument for the "two universalisms" in *Postcolonial Theory and the Specter of Capital* (London: Verso, 2013), chap. 8.

7. Claus Offe and Helmut Wiesenthal, "The Two Logics of Collective Action," *Political Power and Social Theory* 1 (1980): 67–115. This essay remains the foundational analysis of the dilemmas of class formation within capitalism.

8. Offe and Wiesenthal, "The Two Logics of Collective Action," 185–191.

9. For an excellent account of how workers have used such situations to their advantage in class organizing, see Howard Kimeldorf, "Worker Replacement Costs and Unionization: Origins of the U.S. Labor Movement," *American Sociological Review* 78, no. 6 (2013): 1033–1062.

10. Still one of the best discussions of this process is Michael Hechter, *Principles of Group Solidarity* (Berkeley: University of California Press, 1987). A recent examination of how solidarity has been achieved in diverse work settings is Margaret Levi and John Ahlquist, *In the Interest of Others: Organizations and Social Activism* (Princeton, NJ: Princeton University Press, 2013).

3. Consent, Coercion, and Resignation

1. The lectures were only recently published as Stuart Hall, *Cultural Studies 1983: A Theoretical History* (Durham, NC: Duke University Press, 2016).

2. Hall, *Cultural Studies 1983*, 5, emphasis in original.

3. Hall, *Cultural Studies 1983*, 7.

4. Hall, *Cultural Studies 1983*, 7–8.

5. Hall, *Cultural Studies 1983*, 22.

6. Hall, *Cultural Studies 1983*, 24. See also pages 21–23 generally for his fuller description of the challenge.

7. Noberto Bobbio, "Gramsci and the Conception of Civil Society," in *Gramsci and Marxist Theory*, ed. Chantal Mouffe (London: Routledge, 1979), 21–47.

8. See the discussion, with references, in Perry Anderson's pathbreaking study, "The Antinomies of Antonio Gramsci," *New Left Review* 100 (1977): 5–77.

9. Martin Carnoy, *The State and Political Theory* (Princeton, NJ: Princeton University Press, 1985), 69, 70. Emphasis added.

10. The basic polarity between coercion and consent in Marxist theory is explored in John Hoffman, *The Gramscian Challenge: Coercion and Consent in Marxist Political Theory* (London: Basil Blackwell, 1984).

11. Elizabeth Anderson, *Private Government: How Employers Rule Our Lives (and Why We Don't Talk About It)* (Princeton, NJ: Princeton University Press, 2017).

12. Some relevant literature for the importance of these grievances is examined in Richard Hyman, *Strikes*, 4th ed. (London: Macmillan, 1989), chaps. 4–5.

13. Louis Althusser, "Ideology and the Ideological State Apparatuses," in *Lenin and Philosophy and Other Essays* (New York: Monthly Review Press, 1972), 23–71.

14. See the essays in Adam Przeworski, *Capitalism and Social Democracy* (Cambridge: Cambridge University Press, 1985), esp. chap. 4.

15. Przeworski, *Capitalism and Social Democracy*, 135.

16. Przeworski, *Capitalism and Social Democracy*, 136–137.

17. Przeworski, *Capitalism and Social Democracy*, 145–148.

18. For some important examples of this alternative trend, see Joseph Femia, *Gramsci's Political Theory* (Clarendon, UK: Oxford University Press, 1981); Peter Ghosh, "Gramscian Hegemony: An Absolute Historicist Approach," *History of European Ideas* 27 (2001): 1–43; and Michael Burawoy, "For a Sociological Marxism: The Complementary Convergence of Antonio Gramsci and Karl Polanyi," *Politics and Society* 31, no. 2 (June 2003): 193–261. An excellent text, which has been largely ignored, is Peter Gibbon, "Gramsci, Eurocommunism and the Comintern," *Economy and Society* 12, no. 3 (1983): 328–366.

19. Antonio Gramsci, *Selections from the Prison Notebooks*, trans. and ed. Quentin Hoare and Quentin Nowell Smith (New York: International Publishers, 1971), 161, emphasis added.

20. Gramsci, *Selections from the Prison Notebooks*, 12, emphasis added.

21. Gramsci, *Selections from the Prison Notebooks*, 182.

22. Gramsci, *Selections from the Prison Notebooks*, 181.

23. Gramsci, *Selections from the Prison Notebooks*, 460; see also 106, 138, 162, 177.

24. Gramsci, *Selections from the Prison Notebooks*, 177.

25. Gramsci, *Selections from the Prison Notebooks*, 106. This is a much closer approximation of Marx's original. The relevant passage in Marx is the following: "No

social formation ever perishes before all the productive forces for which there is room in it have developed; and new, higher relations of production never appear before the material conditions of their existence have matured in the womb of the old society itself. Therefore mankind always sets itself only such tasks as it can solve; since, looking at the matter more closely, it will always be found that the task itself arises only when the material conditions for its solution already exist or are at least in the process of formation." See Karl Marx, preface to *A Contribution to a Critique of Political Economy* (Moscow: Progress Publishers, 1970).

26. See Gramsci, *Selections from the Prison Notebooks*, 177–185. These pages are probably the most important in the entire English translation of the *Notebooks*.

27. There is also the possibility of its translating into reductions in working time, but that has turned out to be quite rare and, if it happens at all, requires a very high level of class organization, making it less reliable as a source of consent.

28. See Sections 2.1 and 3.3.

29. See the excellent survey in Chris Nyland, *Reduced Worktime and the Management of Production* (Cambridge: Cambridge University Press, 1989), 37–66.

30. See Leopold Haimson and Charles Tilly, eds., *Strikes, Wars and Revolutions in an International Perspective: Strike Waves in the Late Nineteenth and Early Twentieth Centuries* (Cambridge: Cambridge University Press, 1989).

31. See Robert Brenner, "The Political Economy of the Rank and File Rebellion," in *Rebel Rank and File: Labor Militancy and Revolt from Below During the Long 1970s*, ed. Aaron Brenner, Robert Brenner, and Cal Winslow (London: Verso, 2010), 37–76, esp. 51–62.

32. Gramsci, *Selections from the Prison Notebooks*, 263.

33. Gramsci, *Selections from the Prison Notebooks*, 275–276.

34. Gramsci described such a situation as an "interregnum," in which "morbid symptoms appear." Interregnums are temporary states—they mark the transition from one state to another. The morbidity was only additional evidence that the existing order's time was up—that sooner or later, the challengers would come together and install a new order. See Gramsci, *Selections from the Prison Notebooks*, 275–276.

35. For the United States, see the Economic Policy Institute, "Understanding the Historic Divergence between Productivity and the Typical Worker's Pay," Briefing Paper #406, 2015; for Germany, see Oliver Nachtwey, *Germany's Hidden*

Crisis (London: Verso, 2018), chaps. 3 and 4; for Britain, see Simon Mohun, "Britain: From the Golden Age to an Age of Austerity," *Catalyst: A Journal of Theory and Strategy* 3, no. 2 (2019): 65–109.

36. Karl Marx and Frederick Engels, *Collected Works, Vol. 35: Capital: A Critique of Political Economy, Volume 1* (Moscow: Progress Publishers, 1995), 726.

37. Gramsci, *Selections from the Prison Notebooks*, 299.

38. Goran Therborn, *The Ideology of Power and the Power of Ideology* (London: Verso, 1980), 17. While Therborn's argument is heavily influenced by Althusser, it exhibits none of the latter's functionalism.

4. Agency, Contingency, and All That

1. William Sewell, *The Logics of History* (Chicago: University of Chicago Press, 2005), 125.

2. See Karl Marx, *Capital*, vol. 1 (New York: Vintage, 1976), 375, 377, 449, and 557 as examples. The book is strewn with the expression.

3. A foundational argument in contemporary philosophy is Donald Davidson, "Actions, Reasons and Causes," *Journal of Philosophy* 60, no. 23 (1963): 685–700. For a useful overview of the issues involved, see Carlos Moya, *The Philosophy of Action: An Introduction* (London: Polity Press, 1990).

4. Dipesh Chakrabarty, *Provincializing Europe* (Princeton, NJ: Princeton University Press, 2000), 95. But see also his more general argument on pages 47–71.

5. Chakrabarty uses the metaphor of a waiting room to describe this attitude. Regions that do not fit into the predicted institutional design are treated as if they are in a waiting room so that, after an allotted period of time, they will be granted access to the end state predicted by the theory. Chakrabarty, *Provincializing Europe*, 8–10, 65.

6. Engels's dubious contribution was to offer up the caveat that *sometimes* the superstructure was able to escape the direct influence of the base and even react back onto it. But all this did was turn the theory into a tautology—the base determines the superstructure, except in those instances in which it doesn't.

7. See G. A. Cohen, "Restricted and Inclusive Historical Materialism," in *History, Labour and Freedom: Themes from Marx* (Oxford: Oxford University Press, 1988), 155–179.

8. See Cohen, "Restricted and Inclusive Historical Materialism."

9. This argument rests on a deeper critique of Cohen's defense of classical historical materialism, as well as Erik Olin Wright's reconstruction of it. See my "What Is Living and What Is Dead in the Marxist Theory of History," *Historical Materialism* 19, no. 2 (2011): 60–91.

10. See Fred Block, "Varieties of What? Should We Still Be Using the Concept of Capitalism?" *Political Power and Social Theory* 23 (2012): 271–293, and Fred Block, *Capitalism: The Future of an Illusion* (Berkeley: University of California Press, 2018), 1–15.

11. Some key works on the social democratic road are Andrew Shonfield, *Modern Capitalism: The Changing Balance of Public and Private Power* (Oxford: Oxford University Press, 2965); Gosta Esping-Andersen, *Politics against Markets: The Social Democratic Road to Power* (Princeton, NJ: Princeton University Press, 1985); Gosta Esping-Andersen, *The Three Worlds of Welfare Capitalism* (Princeton, NJ: Princeton University Press, 1990); and Jonas Pontusson, *The Limits of Social Democracy: Investment Politics in Sweden* (Princeton, NJ: Princeton University Press, 1992).

12. For comparisons, see Jonas Pontusson, *Inequality and Prosperity: Social Europe versus Liberal America* (Ithaca, NY: Cornell University Press, 2005), and Lane Kenworthy, *Social Democratic Capitalism* (Oxford: Oxford University Press, 2020).

13. The Soviet Union lasted from 1917 to 1989, but the centralized planning system was only constructed after 1928, giving its economic life span a much shorter duration.

14. See the sources in footnote 11. Also Walter Korpi, *The Democratic Class Struggle* (London: Routledge, 1983); John D. Stephens, *The Transition from Capitalism to Socialism* (New Haven, CT: Yale University Press, 1979); Patrick Emmenegger, *The Power to Dismiss: Trade Unions and the Regulation of Job Security in Western Europe* (London: Routledge, 2014); and Thomas Paster, *The Role of Business in the Development of the Welfare State and Labor Markets in Germany* (London: Routledge, 2012).

15. See Thomas Ferguson, "From 'Normalcy' to New Deal: Industrial Structure, Party Competition, and American Public Policy in the Great Depression," *International Organization* 38, no. 1 (winter 1984): 41–94; Michael Goldfield, "Worker Insurgency, Radical Organization, and New Deal Labor Legislation," *American Political Science Review* 83, no. 4 (December 1989): 1257–1282; J. Craig Jenkins and Barbara G. Brents, "Social Protest, Hegemonic Competition, and Social

Reform: A Political Struggle Interpretation of the Origins of the American Welfare State," *American Sociological Review* 54, no. 6 (December 1989): 891–909; and Colin Gordon, *New Deals: Business, Politics and Labor in America, 1920–1935* (Cambridge: Cambridge University Press, 1995).

16. The key work here was Peter Hall and David Soskice, *Varieties of Capitalism: The Institutional Foundations of Comparative Advantage* (Oxford: Oxford University Press, 2001). The literature associated with this stream of research is enormous. For overviews, see Kathleen Thelen, "Varieties of Capitalism: Trajectories of Liberalization and the New Politics of Social Solidarity," *Annual Review of Political Science* 15 (2012): 137–159, and Magnus Feldmann, "Global Varieties of Capitalism," *World Politics* 71, no. 1 (January 2019): 162–196.

17. Chris Howell and Lucio Bacarro, *Trajectories of Neoliberal Transformation: European Industrial Relations Since the 1970s* (Cambridge: Cambridge University Press, 2017). The countries they examine are Britain, France, Germany, Italy, and Sweden.

18. See the data in Kathleen Thelen, *Varieties of Liberalization and the New Politics of Solidarity* (Cambridge: Cambridge University Press, 2014), 35, Tables 2.3 and 2.4.

19. For Britain, see Chris Howell, *Trade Unions and the State: Constructing Industrial Relations Institutions in Britain, 1890–2000* (Princeton, NJ: Princeton University Press, 2005); Alexander Gallas, *The Thatcherite Offensive: A Neo-Poulantzian Analysis* (Leiden, Netherlands: Brill, 2016); and Richard Vinen, "A War of Position? The Thatcherite Government's Preparation for the 1984 Miners' Strike," *English Historical Review* (2020); for France, see Chris Howell, "The French Road to Neoliberalism," *Catalyst: A Journal of Theory and Strategy* 2, no. 3 (2018): 83–122; Bruno Amable, *Structural Crisis and Institutional Change in Modern Capitalism: French Capitalism in Transition* (Oxford: Oxford University Press, 2017), chap. 3; and Bruno Amable, "The Political Economy of the Neoliberal Transformation of French Industrial Relations," *ILR Review* 69, no. 3 (May 2016): 523–550.

20. Peter Swenson and Jonas Pontusson, "Labor Markets, Production Strategies, and Wage Bargaining Institutions: The Swedish Employer Offensive in Comparative Perspective," *Comparative Political Studies* 29, no. 2 (April 1996): 223–250; Peter Swenson and Jonas Pontusson, "The Swedish Employer Offensive against Centralized Wage Bargaining," in *Unions, Employers and Central Banks: Macroeconomic Coordination and Institutional Change in Social Market Economies,* ed. Torben

Iversen, Jonas Pontusson and David Soskice (Cambridge: Cambridge University Press, 2000).

21. For the employer reaction to reunification, see Lowell Turner, *Fighting for Partnership: Labor and Politics in Unified Germany* (Ithaca, NY: Cornell University Press, 1998); for the early 2000s and beyond, see Daniel Kinderman, "Pressure from Without, Subversion from Within: The Two-Pronged German Employer Offensive," *Comparative European Politics* 3 (2005): 432–463, and Thomas Paster, "Do German Employers Support Board-Level Codetermination? The Paradox of Individual Support and Collective Opposition," *Socio-Economic Review* 10 (2012): 471–495. A general analysis is in Oliver Nachtwey, *Germany's Hidden Crisis* (London: Verso, 2018), and Oliver Nachtwey and Loren Balhorn, "Berlin Is Not (Yet) Weimar: The Federal Republic in Protracted Decline," *Catalyst: A Journal of Theory and Strategy* 2, no. 4 (winter 2018–2019): 41–80.

22. Goran Therborn, "Twilight of Swedish Social Democracy," *New Left Review* 113 (September–October 2018): 9.

23. Jonas Pontusson, "Unions, Inequality, and Redistribution," *British Journal of Industrial Relations* 51, no. 4 (December 2013): 798.

24. Evelyn Huber, Jingjing Huo, and John D. Stephens, "Power, Policy, and Top Income Shares," *Socio-Economic Review* 17, no. 2 (2019): 248. For a general review of the literature, which broadly supports the findings of Huber, Huo, and Stephens and Pontusson, see Sandy Hager, "Varieties of Top Income Shares," *Socio-Economic Review* 18, no. 4 (October 2020): 1175–1198, esp. 18–19.

25. Howell and Bacarro, *Trajectories of Neoliberal Transformation*, chaps. 2 and 3.

5. How Capitalism Endures

1. For Europe, see Goran Therborn, "The Rule of Capital and the Rise of Democracy," *New Left Review* 103 (May–June 1977): 3–42; for the United States, see Walter Dean Burnham, "The Appearance and Disappearance of the American Voter," in *The Political Economy: Readings in the Politics and Economics of American Public Policy,* ed. Thomas Ferguson and Joel Rogers (New York: M. E. Sharpe, 1984), 112–139.

2. Ira Katznelson, *Marxism and the City* (Oxford: Oxford University Press, 1993), 214–218; David Gordon, "Capitalist Development and the History of American

Cities," in *Marxism and the Metropolis,* ed. Tabb (1984), 35–36; Richard Harris, "Residential Segregation and Class Formation in the Capitalist City," 33–34.

3. The classic statement is T. H. Marshall's 1950 essay, "Citizenship and Social Class," reprinted in *Citizenship and Social Class,* ed. Tom Bottomore (London: Pluto Press, 1992).

4. I have in mind the "varieties of capitalism" school, discussed briefly in Chapter 4.

5. The literature on the economic stagnation of the 1970s is enormous. For the connection between the economic slowdown and its connection to employer strategy toward unions and social democracy, see Robert Brenner, *The Economics of Global Turbulence* (London: Verso, 2006), and David Kotz, *The Rise and Fall of Neoliberal Capitalism* (Cambridge, MA: Harvard University Press, 2018).

6. The key research on this has been carried out by Thomas Piketty, Emmanuel Saez, and their colleagues. See, inter alia, Emmanuel Saez, "Income and Wealth Inequality: Evidence and Policy Implications," *Contemporary Economic Policy* 35, no. 1 (January 2017): 7–25. On trends in wealth inequality in particular, see Edward N. Wolff's recent opus, *A Century of Wealth in America* (Cambridge, MA: Harvard University Press, 2017).

7. Anne Case and Angus Deaton, *Deaths of Despair and the Future of Capitalism* (Princeton, NJ: Princeton University Press, 2020).

8. TINA famously was an acronym for "there is no alternative."

9. As noted by none other than the chairman of the Federal Reserve, Alan Greenspan, "heightened job insecurity is the most significant explanation" of the timidity of US labor, a development so dramatic that he characterized it as a "break with the past." See Greenspan's testimony to the Senate Committee on Banking, Housing, and Urban Affairs, February 26, 1997, accessed June 13, 2021, https://www.federalreserve.gov/boarddocs/hh/1997/february/testimony.htm; see also Alan Krueger, "Reflections on Dwindling Worker Bargaining Power and Monetary Policy," August 24, 2018, Luncheon Address at the Jackson Hole Economic Symposium, available at https://www.kansascityfed.org/~/media/files/publicat/sympos/2018/papersandhandouts/824180824kruegerremarks.pdf?la=en.

10. Benjamin Page and Lawrence Jacobs, *Class War: What Americans Really Think about Economic Inequality* (Chicago: Chicago University Press, 2009); Leslie McCall,

The Undeserving Rich: American Beliefs about Inequality, Opportunity and Redistribution (Cambridge: Cambridge University Press, 2013).

11. In 2018 alone, the number of workers involved in stoppages was the most since 1986, and the strikes in 2019 exceeded that number. See Bureau of Labor Statistics (BLS), "Work Stoppages Summary," February 11, 2020, https://www.bls.gov/news.release/wkstp.nr0.htm.

12. The BLS reports that in 2010–2019, the private sector experienced 93 stoppages while state and local workers accounted for 61. BLS, "Work Stoppages Summary."

13. For deindustrialization in the advanced world, a seminal text was Robert Rowthorn and J. E. Wells, *Deindustrialization and Foreign Trade* (Cambridge: Cambridge University Press, 1987); for a longer sweep, see Charles Feinstein, "Structural Change in the Developed Countries during the Twentieth Century," *Oxford Review of Economic Policy* 15, no. 4 (1999). For early deindustrialization, see Dani Rodrik, "Premature Deindustrialization," *Journal of Economic Growth* 21 (2016): 1–33.

14. See the brilliant description of the changes in workplace relations today compared to a half century ago in David Weil, *The Fissured Workplace: Why Work Became So Bad for So Many and What Can Be Done to Improve It* (Cambridge, MA: Harvard University Press, 2014).

15. Eric Hobsbawm, "Labour and the Great City," *New Left Review* 166 (November–December 1987): 48–49. See also Katznelson, *Marxism and the City.*

16. Thomas Piketty, *Capital and Ideology* (Cambridge, MA: Harvard University Press, 2020), chaps. 14–16.

Acknowledgments

The impetus for this book derived in large part from reactions to my previous one. After the release of *Postcolonial Theory and the Specter of Capital* in 2013, friends and colleagues noted that my arguments rested on a materialist class theory that was only presented in bits and pieces. What was needed was a fuller explication of that underlying theory of class and capitalism, which turned out to be this book. The call was made most forcefully by Michael Schwartz, but also Jeff Goodwin and Bashir Abu-Manneh. A somewhat impromptu lecture in Zagreb in November 2016 allowed me to present some of the central arguments, and I would like to thank the organizers of the event. I would especially like to thank Stipe Curkovic, whose intervention at the event was not only very helpful in its own right but enabled me to more clearly formulate some of my arguments.[*]

My colleagues Iddo Tavory and Paul Dimaggio very generously invited me to present some core propositions to their Cultural Theory workshop at NYU, for which I am grateful, and especially to the two of them for their very helpful

---

[*] The lecture and discussion can be viewed on YouTube at https://www.youtube.com /watch?v=2dcVoQbhFtQ.

comments. A presentation at Harvard University's History, Culture, and Society workshop in March 2020, organized by Orlando Patterson and Ya-wen Lei, was also tremendously useful, especially the interventions by Alex Lichtenstein. Once the final manuscript was ready, Jeff Goodwin organized a Zoom workshop around it, where Steven Lukes, Adaner Usmani, and Jeremy Cohan presented searching critiques of the arguments. These were bolstered by interventions from many of the participants. I want to thank, in no particular order, Niall Reddy, Virgilio Urbina Lazardi, Nada Matta, Suzy Lee, Rene Rojas, Chris Maisano, Neal Meyer, Mark Cohen, and Daniel Cheng for their comments. Daniel in particular made a crucial suggestion for a diagram in Chapter 1, which helped improve the presentation, and Virgilio spotted a critical conceptual ambiguity prompting some rewriting. I was delighted when Roberto Veneziani offered to read the manuscript, and even more so at the care and thoroughness with which he put it to the scalpel. I have tried my best to correct the many weaknesses and errors he pointed out, at least enough so that he might suppose that it wasn't a complete waste of his time.

For ongoing conversations, reactions, and general moral support, I am grateful to my "kitchen cabinet" of Nivedita Majumdar, Bashir Abu Manneh, and Jeff Goodwin. The many students in my PhD courses, especially the extraordinary group of students at NYU, were not only supportive of the effort, but through their participation in my seminars and workshops over the years, played an integral role in the book's development. So too the friends and colleagues at the Center for Marxist Studies in Delhi, especially Achin Vanaik, Willy D'Costa, and Archana Aggarwal. Many of the book's arguments were developed in lectures at the school's semi-annual meetings.

I have been very fortunate to have had Ian Malcolm as an editor not once, but twice. He is the consummate professional—supportive, enthusiastic, patient, and always responsive. I am once again grateful to him for shepherding this project to completion. And also to two anonymous reviewers for Harvard University Press for their very astute comments.

My biggest regret is that Erik Olin Wright did not live to see the book to completion. No intellectual did more to develop materialist class theory in the postwar era than Erik, and this book builds directly on his own work. His untimely death is an enormous blow to the academic world at large, but an especially painful one to me personally and intellectually. We discussed almost every idea in this book at some time or the other. Thankfully, he did get to respond to the core arguments in Chapters 1 and 2, which I first presented in my article "Rescuing Class from the Cultural Turn," *Catalyst* 1, no. 1 (Spring 2017): 27–56, parts of which appear in these chapters. But I did not have the benefit of his extraordinary mind when the project was completed. I owe more to him than I could ever convey, and lovingly dedicate this book to his memory.

Index